CRACKING
THE MONOLITH

CRACKING THE MONOLITH

• • • THE STRUGGLE
FOR THE SOUL OF AMERICA

A Peace and Justice Manifesto

WILLIAM W. RANKIN

*to Hannah Lawrence Schuller
with great appreciation
for your friendship.
Bill Rankin
Dec. 16, 1997*

CROSSROAD ▪ NEW YORK

1994
The Crossroad Publishing Company
370 Lexington Avenue, New York, NY 10017

Printed in the United States of America

The Author wishes to thank the following for permission to quote from previously published material: Carcanet Press Limited for *The Mystery of the Charity of Joan of Arc* by Charles Peguy, adaptation copyright © Jean-Paul Lucet 1983, translation copyright © Jeffrey Wainwright 1984, 1986, afterword copyright © Marina Warner 1986.

Library of Congress Cataloging-in-Publication Data

Rankin, William W., 1941–
    Cracking the monolith : the struggle for the soul of America : a
peace and justice manifesto / William W. Rankin.
        p.   cm.
    Includes bibliographical references.
    ISBN 0-8245-1439-4
    1. Christianity and justice.   2. Peace—Religious aspects—
Christianity.   3. Leadership—Religious aspects—Christianity.
4. Church and social problems—United States.   I. Title.
BR115.J8R32   1994
261.8′00973—dc20   94–21235
                                                        CIP

To Sally Heller Rankin,

sine qua non,

and

The Reverend Brian Jervis Grieves,

servant of Christ

CONTENTS

INTRODUCTION

M y novelist friend Anne Lamott once referred to the remote centers of political power, seemingly impenetrable and aloof, as "the monolith." She had in mind an image of a place, or constellation of locations, in our country where the wealthy importune the powerful, and decisions are made that structure society to the advantage of the privileged and the disadvantage of others.

A monolith, literally, is a single stone; as a metaphor for impassive power, the term evokes shades of Kafka. Feelings of helplessness before this are all but inevitable. Unchallenged, however, they induce our collusion with the status quo. We need, instead, active engagement with the justice- and peacemaking imperatives central to the Christian affirmation.

A large stone, for all its inertia, invites the architect or sculptor to begin the long, faithful commitment to create a thing of nobility and beauty, of humane consequence. The confrontation with the monolith leads to a first act, followed by many more. Confident in the animating Spirit of God, Christians especially possess a moral and spiritual resource to move from stultification to creation—of the right and good, the lovely and the true.

When Arthur M. Schlesinger, Jr., wrote his testament to John F. Kennedy, he said, "Above all he gave the world for an imperishable moment the vision of a leader who greatly understood the terror and the hope, the diversity and the possibility, of life on this planet and who made people look beyond nation and race to the future of humanity."[1] Intuitively the world knew, and knows, the importance of sound leadership. That Christians have a crucial leadership role to play in the church and in the "secular world" has been rightly and insistently proclaimed in lay ministry circles for a long time. It is also a recently rediscovered emphasis in the renewed appreciation for the deacon's ministry. Having been a parish priest for over a quarter century, and now the president of a seminary, I am interested in the question of Christian leadership—particularly the matter of faithfulness to certain major themes of the Bible, like the great issues of peace- and justice-making. This concern by no means has been limited to the context of the institutional church; it is also with the quality of leadership given to the larger society, which I believe Christians could enhance by way of attending to the peace and justice accents of our religious heritage. This book attempts to advance a Christian social ethics–based understanding of leadership for laity and clergy, in both church and society.

What one finds written on the subject of leadership tends to fall into the business and economics category, where profit maximization is a presiding consideration, or into studies emphasizing the psychological well-being of personnel. Churches and their leaders have much to learn from sources like these, and we should take them very much to heart. But it is also conceivable that a given church is doing well financially, that its constituency is well pleased, and still it is not being faithful to its higher ethical calling as a Christian community. I believe that calling has to do with all the things we normally associate with church life, including worship and pastoring, of course, but it must also include faithfulness in the matters of peace and justice.[2]

Leaders in the church and in the larger society are in especially important positions because, precisely as leaders, they tend to have closer access to the levers of decision-making and implementation than the rest of us do. They tend to influence, as also they respond to, public opinion. While this seems obvious enough, it is not to say that top-down leadership is, or should be, always determinative or even significantly efficacious in our somewhat democratic society; in many ways important initiatives will always be taken by individuals and local groups, regardless of what some remoter authority presumes to legislate. The present point is simply that as a general rule we have, after all, settled upon leadership as a phenomenon, in whatever ways it is construed and authorized at particular levels of social organization. This means we have in fact assigned a certain amount of authority to leaders, however elected or appointed, in various social contexts in which we operate—in churches or other membership organizations, in our job context, and at community, state, and federal levels.

A premise of this book is that if leaders at *all* levels of social organization better understood and took more to heart the particular biblical themes of *shalom*, communality, and sociality, our lives together would be in better alignment with what the Bible indicates is the mind—perhaps the caring heart—of God. In this book actual leadership practice is examined to analyze what is indeed occurring, to discover some of its salient problems, and to see what is required instead to bring about outcomes more consistent with Christian moral imperatives.

The seriousness with which we attend to one or another aspect of our societal life with each other is an important variable. Someone has said that we tend to get the leaders we deserve. Our society and its institutions are at least nuanced by the leaders we in some degree have allowed to influence them. With respect to some of us in particular, policies enacted by political leaders are consequential indeed—over 37 million Americans have no health insurance, for example. What is needed is a stimulus to thought concerning leadership—in the church and at all levels of our organized life together—from a Christian ethics point of view.

It is worth saying, too, that *all* Christians should be playing leadership roles in some way or other—as opinion leaders, advocates, analysts, critics, or whatnot—even if we are not otherwise formally elected or appointed as such. So when leadership is under discussion in the chapters following, it will be evident from the context that I am at one moment referring to formally identified leaders, and at another moment to all Christians, whom I would like to see assuming leadership roles for just and peaceable institutions in a just and peaceable society.

The test of a faithful church, and of Christian leadership in general, is how well we are witnessing to the sovereignty of God, and God's Christ, in this imperfect world. We are supposed to witness to divine goodness, mercy, compassion, respect for all, and so forth. But this also means watching—being on guard against their opposites: such things as individual and social malevolence, meanness, exploitation, exclusion, enmity, prejudice (in matters of race and gender, for example), and, generally, injustice, because the weak in society, who from a Christian perspective need especially to be protected, can end up being the most hurt. From the perspective of the foot of the cross—the victim's point of view—this social condition is simply wrong. A sincere determination to recognize, understand, and respond by witnessing and watching is desperately needed from all sorts of leaders these days, Christian or otherwise.

A familiar difficulty, of course, is that leadership positions, being usually elected or appointed, have not predictably been filled with people who care immediately about the greater issues of social ethics. This may largely be due to the fact that many of the rest of us have assigned too low a priority to these tough matters; we have tended, somewhat understandably, to be absorbed with more immediate concerns, and these are what we press upon our leaders. Correspondingly, especially if they feel answerable to a relatively privileged population, formal leaders tend not to trouble their constituencies with the great and sometimes anguishing matters of social justice.[3]

Being a faithful leader, or a plain old person, concerned with the social ethics issues of the day is not easy; but the alternative—defaulting in that kind of responsibility—suggests the possibility that a person of the Bible actually doesn't understand what that book says. It says that God's particular commitment is to those who have little or no inherent protections in society. This is why the "widows and orphans" (husbandless women and fatherless children, who had no inherent rights in a male-dominated society) and "sojourners" (people without citizenship rights) are insistently shown to be under God's special protection. Exploiting the weak in society brings the offender(s), and the entire society, into very serious trouble with God—which can be seen most pointedly in the remark of Jesus that if anyone caused hurt to a "little one," his or her prospects would be less than for someone thrown into the sea tied to a millstone.

The Christian statement in the New Testament is about our all being saved and reconciled to God and to each other. And it is about the availability to us of God's Spirit to help us embody that truth, and its implications, in our daily lives. The biblical motive for my response to the plight of the weak is not thus to achieve my salvation by good works—this is already accomplished as a divine gift—but instead to recognize gratefully that the God who loves privileged people loves the weak too, and that because of their vulnerability they are in particular need of our concern. When the socially vulnerable have no hope in this world, their hope must be in God; as God's people, we embody God's commitment ("preferential option," it has been called) to those who especially need it.

My hope is that some of the proposals in the present work will stimulate thinking, and perhaps fortify a climate within which a certain way of being faithful to God and to the vulnerable is more likely. So the present concern is not with the tactics of local congregational management. Strategy and tactics, after all, are best worked out in the uniqueness of a particular context, and every situation is different. Instead, here is an exploration into some elements of the violence and injustice predicaments of our time, concerning which leadership in any venue is urgently needed.

QUO VADIS?

An essential question for leaders is, In which direction are we supposed to lead? It is difficult to apply to the conditions of this world a precise blueprint of the Kingdom for which Jesus taught us to pray, and thus indicate unequivocally what is right and wrong, desirable and undesirable, about various of our current social alternatives, visions, and goals. Yet there are clues in the biblical record for what is socially desirable. I am simplifying this matter by appropriating here a useful differentiation between the modern and postmodern worlds. I am borrowing from some good work by David Ray Griffin.[4] My premise is that his view is correct, and that what is undesirable from a Christian point of view are the values and vision implicit in the modern world. What is desirable are the values and vision of the postmodern world, as Griffin defines these terms.

He characterizes a world that he hopes we are leaving behind. It is animated, he says, by an arrogant, smug, imperialistic, self-aggrandizing psychology. It is masculine *cum* macho in terms of its driving spirituality, according high regard to individualism, centralization, industrialization, urbanization, automation, racism (despite official rhetoric to the contrary), and nationalism. In the modern world, materialism, classism, competition, and environmental degradation all bedevil us to an increasingly unpleasant degree. "The birth of the modern nation-state, the rapacious Industrial Revolution, and the horror of modern warfare on a global scale have all contributed to 'the modern condition,'" he writes. "We have lost the security of an intact world and a sense of our place in the cosmos. . . . Clinging to the illusions of modern rationality, we are careening with entirely illogical motions toward species suicide."[5]

In such a state of affairs, the quality of our lives is diminishing steadily. Our main need is for a unified alternative vision to the stultifying rat race. For Griffin, the main pillars of demonic modernism, which need to be transcended in constructing this alternative, are "the state as a focus for political loyalty, nationalism as a mobilizing ideology, the market as a basis for allocating resources, war potential as the fulcrum of international stability, and nuclear weapons as providing the only deterrence capable of avoiding world war. . . ."[6]

Cultural modernism has been intertwined with modern theologies—early and late modern theologies. The former is seen most clearly in eighteenth-century deism, which sought, as he put it, "to accommodate theology to the modern worldview by reducing theology's content."[7] Late modern theology "conceded the arena of public discourse to the modern worldview" and retreated to the private realm of interior, individual faith and personal piety—apart from any direct relevance to the public realm at all.[8] Consistent with this, modern spirituality takes little or no account of the fact that individuals are related to others and to their environment, and that in this relatedness inhere obligations. The consequence for modern spirituality is the increasing isolation of people, their morbid competition with one another, and the fertile ground for theories of social Darwinism—the notion that the fittest in society deservedly and "naturally" flourish, whereas the others "naturally" do not survive and do not deserve to.[9] Social Darwinism rationalizes the neglect, possibly the antipathy, of its devotees concerning the vulnerable; this is a demon that drives the spirituality of violence and injustice.

The end of confidence in the modern world is upon at least some of us. Someone more glib than I might announce this as an aspect of God's judgment against modernism's failures—especially its failures in the peace and justice areas. Whether or not it is divine judgment, a widespread disillusionment with human progress has nonetheless set in. With it has come a corresponding skepticism of certain religious affirmations and of religious authority. Skepticism of the capacity of science and technology to deliver us to a bright future increases daily, as does our worry over the stability of the environment against continued insults from humankind. Doubts grow over favorable prospects for large groups of the chronically ill, children, and impoverished people, and over the safety of thousands of weapons of mass destruction that still lurk in the arsenals of several nations, to name just a few examples.

From this slough of despond arises a hope, or a vision, or perhaps a paradigm for a new way of conceiving our future. The term frequently used to connote this is "postmodern." For the present purpose, borrowing from David Griffin, it means "a diffuse sentiment rather than . . . any common set of doctrines—the sentiment that humanity can and must go beyond the modern."[10] This is a constructive attempt to envision the world, and humankind, in a unified way that places more emphasis upon relationships among people than the achievements of individuals, women and men together with equal valuation, respect for people without reference to their age or health status, or their producing or purchasing power; it means nonviolent reconciliation more than solving problems by force, ecology, fairness, communality, human and animal liberation, and the theology, ethics, and spirituality that are compatible with these things. These things, we might reasonably infer from our reading of the Bible, and our understanding of God throughout church history, are desirable from a divine point of view. They lie at the center of most Christian feminist theologies.

For all this, however, postmodernism is not utopian; it accepts the teachings of both the Jewish and Christian religions that there are, and will be, fundamental flaws at the heart of the human condition. In a world where violence is inevitable, for instance, force will still be needed for rigorously justified self-defense. From this recognition comes the awareness that struggle will always be needed, and that even those (*especially* those) who think they are doing the right and good may still have things dreadfully wrong. In consideration of this, the corrective of Christian community, in dialogue with the insights of the larger tradition, is recognized as a guard and guide for any one among us.

But the postmodern vision at least sets a general direction for leaders and all of us; it provides, even if vaguely, a moral compass. Things that incline toward the liberation of society's oppressed people for full and equal participation are probably good. So are things that enhance global security and solidarity, things that empower people at community levels to participate in shaping their own destinies, that promote nonviolence, that respect diversity, and that recognize God as a creative nurturer and reconciler, rather than an overbearing, stern, hotblooded, tribal chieftain.

An implication of the postmodern theological sensibility is that people and God are thought of in relational terms; with other feminists I construe God as a Divine Presence among us rather than as utterly removed from us in the older sense of "infinite qualitative distinction." Moreover, in this scheme God does not continue as the tribal deity of one part of humankind only; rather, God is the God of all, in some degree present to all and knowable by all. The male Jesus of history of course stands as a central reference point for Christians, but the Christ of faith is the liberating, inclusive, nurturing, feminine, community-building spirit of God discovered whenever the peaceable Kingdom of God is made manifest in human affairs.[11] In the realm of ethics, justice directly implies liberation of any who are oppressed by social, economic, racial, gender, or sexual-orientation discrimination; ethics implies ongoing struggle for reconciliation and justice in these kinds of areas. And spirituality is concerned with the motivating power that animates and sustains these sorts of commitments.

■ ■ ■

I would like to say something more about the theological premises of this book. Recall the biblical motifs of witness and watchman. As these terms were used in the ancient Near East they may have had more of a social connotation than they do in our more individualistic culture. But still we know what they mean. For instance, the *San Francisco Chronicle* has a "Question Man" column, in which people interviewed on the street answer a particular question for the day. To the question, "What was the biggest sacrifice you ever made?" a ninety-one-year-old retired retirement-home desk clerk replied, "It was a privilege, but it was when my mother had a stroke and I gave seven years to her. . . . I went to work . . . and went home every single night. I had no lonesomeness and she did everything she could around the house and I had her support and love."[12] Here is witness, surely, to goodness, faithfulness, sacrifice, and perhaps many other things. Taking the interview only at face value, we might feel admiration for this kindly woman. I am interested, however, in expanding the idea and placing it within a wider cultural context, so that witnessing is conceived as putting first, let's say, the interests of all needy people. The church has to be concerned with vulnerable individuals, but also with the larger social forces that swirl around us and affect the lives of oppressed people rather directly.[13] I am especially interested in our leaders catching on to this concern and embodying it—our formal leaders and Christians.

In our daily lives we are familiar with a watchman too, and easily we can imagine our need for one in certain moments of danger. We may think of someone who guards property, but I have in mind someone who guards life. Consider this true account of a young woman who leaves her home in her father's car. She pauses at an intersection, then turns onto a major boulevard. Suddenly she is blinded by the setting sun in front of her, low on the horizon; its bright rays strike the dirty windshield, rendering it opaque. Just ahead a child begins to cross the street; the watchman has left early for home. A tragedy of enormous suffering is about to occur, involving a number of people and their families.

We know on a personal basis the need for a watchman, but I intend to extend this to our larger social context. I want to examine our need to watch for social policies, and the actions authorized by them, that devastate many lives, only more slowly, "legitimately," and subtly than a blinded driver. We need vigilance by Christian leaders—the formal ones, and all Christians in society. They must help the entire community discover what is dangerous and what needs to be done to protect the welfare especially of the weak.

These themes inform the chapters on health and illness, the fate of children, peacemaking and the predisposition to violence, the problems of justice in community caused by official secrecy and deceit, the arms trade, and the legacy of Manifest Destiny. The primary interest in the health chapter is on the ways in which illness does create the acute danger of social and self-stigmatization, and how it is that a society intending itself as just needs to do right by ill and disabled people. That so many of us are so economically vulnerable to catastrophic illness is surely tied to a $300 billion military budget. The implications for sound leadership in this arena are enormous and, for Christians, compelling.

Children are the victims of both war and oppressive peace. Notoriously they represent the future, but they are even more the present, the here-and-now people of God. To paraphrase a former president and distinguished soldier, every bomb, every bullet, every missile, every submarine, every luxurious pension payment to a retired general is in some sense a theft from the children of poverty. But children cannot vote, nor do they have well-heeled political-action committees lobbying for them. As a group they have virtually no legal rights or, for that matter, access to society. If justice implies mutuality, we should be more mutual with the poorest of our little friends.

Our predisposition to violence is a terrible testimony to our enthrallment to the false gods of race, nation, religious exclusivism, and military might. Here is a familiar social syndrome notoriously manipulated by political leaders and colluded in by church leaders. It is an enormously destructive tendency and calls for vigilance, riskful faithfulness, and leadership by all sincere Christians. I examine this problem in its most recent manifestation for us, which is the Gulf War.

As we are beginning to discover in our own national experience, the corruptions so easily recognized in leadership elsewhere are evident among us—all of us—as well. In addition to the tangible damages resulting from these, there are invisible spiritual dangers, which include fear, cynicism, and an inclination to despair on the part of ordinary people. The minimal trust necessary to sustain a people in community is severely eroded when fraud and secrecy characterize the actions of its leaders, especially on a matter with serious ecological, economic, and health implications. Official secrecy and deceit are examined in a chapter on nuclear-weapons production facilities. In this type of case there is an evident need for scrutiny and warning, but also of witness to a divine investment in mutuality, honesty, and integrity in community. There is an urgent need in this respect for just and honorable leadership—offered by Christians and demanded by them.

The arms trade, with its attendant profiteering, makes wars and violence possible in the first place. The people of the U.S. do not benefit from this trade, except for some directly involved in arms manufacture and sale. Since the intrinsic purpose of a weapon is to threaten, harm, and if necessary kill, arms sales constitute a wicked exchange of blood for money. It seems difficult to approve the magnitude of present-day exchanges from a Christian point of view.

Manifest Destiny's legacy of poverty, classism, oppression, and colonialism—first political, later economic—is striking to discover when one travels beyond the comfortable, and sometimes carefully guarded, precincts of posh "Third World" hotels. The problem is not so much the historical racism and arrogance as it is today's conditions. Our firsthand accounts of visits and interviews in Cuba, Central America, and the Philippines are but surface indications of people and events we shall never forget. To a person, we believe the U.S., which so directly and (in certain respects) so disastrously affected people of other countries, is responsible for alleviating the present consequences of injustice. We especially find racism at the heart of this matter.

■ ■ ■

I have been honored to serve as chair of the Episcopal Church's Standing Commission on Peace with Justice. Much of the material in this book was enabled by the national church's generosity in sending my colleagues and me to such "hot spots," during the past six years, as the Middle East, Central America, the Caribbean, South Africa, and the cordillera of Northern Luzon in the Philippines. In each place we were warmly welcomed by the Anglican Church, and were privileged to observe the church's valiant and frequently riskful ministry of justice and peacemaking.

The Standing Commission on Peace with Justice is a sponsor of this book, and various of its members, staff, and friends have contributed directly to its content. I cite especially written contributions and/or editing help from Anne Shirk, Warren Preece, and Nell Gibson on the materials pertaining to the Manifest Destiny section and its present implications for certain countries in Central America and the Caribbean; Anne Shirk, Edward Lee, Nathaniel Pierce, Gary Cummins, and Lee Davis Thames on the arms-trade piece; and important contributions throughout by the other commissioners and staff: Donald Hart, James Ottley, Robert Sessum, William Anderson, Carolyn Carlburg, Patricia Washburn, Marcy Walsh, and Brian Grieves.

I owe a lot to many other people for the assistance given me while I was writing this book. I am deeply indebted to my friend Anne Lamott for her gracious, committed, and competent help with ideas and writing style. She has given me much time, at considerable cost to her own work as a novelist; she has been an extraordinary counselor and teacher in many of the matters discussed in this book. I have also been enormously helped by two dear friends: Professors Harmon Smith, at Duke University, and Owen Thomas, at the Episcopal Divinity School. Each has made helpful suggestions with those chapters I presumed to bother them with; they should be absolved from responsibility for errors I have made in this project. I am grateful to R. T. Heller of Crossroad Books for his wonderful assistance, and to Jane Gerloff, my wonderful colleague and friend at Episcopal Divinity School.

I thank the Right Reverend Otis Charles, Dr. Fredrica Harris Thompsett, and the faculty of Episcopal Divinity School in Cambridge, Massachusetts, for having invited me to deliver the 1991 Kellogg Lectures, which prompted part of this writing project. I also acknowledge, with gratitude, the kindness of the Reverend Dr. Mark Richardson for inviting me to present some of this material in a lecture sponsored by the Graduate Theological Union's Center for Theology and the Natural Sciences in Berkeley, California. And I also thank the Rev. Dr. Jean Clark and the people of St. Andrew Episcopal Church in Saratoga, California, for inviting me to present other parts of this writing there.

To Sally, Amy, and Rob—our dear children—and my mother and sisters, and to the people of St. Stephen Church, Belvedere, California, and of Episcopal Divinity School, Cambridge, Massachusetts: thank you so much.

William Rankin
Cambridge, Massachusetts
April 1994

CRACKING
THE MONOLITH

JUSTICE AND ILL PEOPLE

I would like all people who think themselves healthy to take this chapter to heart, but especially Christians who are leaders of various sorts in the church and in the world. So much can be done for ill people by health-care professionals, but as the AIDS epidemic in particular reminds us just now, there is much that cannot be done by medical technologies alone. What is needed, especially in cases of chronic or progressive illness and disability, is a better understanding of what things are like for ill people, and a clearer recognition of quality-of-life implications of present social policies and priorities.

I have a personal investment in the matters about to be discussed. In 1974 my life took a decisive turn that began to awaken me to what it might feel like not to be among the successful and confident people in our society; my history from this time on has colored everything else. In that year I was diagnosed with asthma. The difficulty was that no medicine at the time was particularly effective with this condition, except systemic steroids, which can have dire side-effects; you don't want to invite these if you can avoid them. The deeper problem is that any allergic phenomenon means that in some degree your immune system is out of whack. For most people this results only in minimum inconvenience, but for me things became more complex. Within two years I was in the hospital and was being told that a lung-tissue biopsy, coupled with other medical findings, supported a diagnosis of vasculitis, a very serious illness.

In retrospect, the asthma had been but a precursor to a more systemic collagen vascular disease. It might take my life in six months, as I was given to believe. This information induced a quality of fear on top of an underlying sadness, which lasted for another year and a half—though after six months from the onset of vasculitis symptoms, the clinical evidence indicated that by then the physical disease process had "burned itself out." Even after the good news that from a medical standpoint I was out of the woods, I still found myself psychologically unable to make any but the most short-range plans; I couldn't bring myself to believe there would be a future for me. Any twinge of pain, any deviation in my body from perfect health, startled me into thinking that a deadly time bomb was once again ticking inside me. I attended much more diligently than before to our two young children, and I thought a whole lot about some of the things you will read in this chapter.

ILLNESS AND IDENTITY

My first concern is with the psychological, or maybe the spiritual, implications of illness. The most disturbing of these is the assault of illness upon one's identity. The adjustment to thinking of yourself as essentially "damaged goods" is the hardest one you must make, apart from facing your own death. The best propositional statement I ever saw along this line was by Irving Cooper, a renowned neurosurgeon at New York City's St. Barnabas Hospital. Cooper has worked with patients suffering from severe dystonia, a sometimes terribly debilitating and contorting predisposition to muscle spasms that convulse the body and profoundly incapacitate the sufferer. In writing of these chronically neurologically handicapped, Cooper said, "The disease lives in that person. . . . The disease embraces the person, clasps him [sic], they fuse to become the diseased-person. The new person may become more sensitive than before, but he is never, never the same."[1] Never, never the same indeed.

The shift in an individual's identity from a person normally unconscious of health to the new identity, a "diseased-person," may entail a qualitative psychological leap of enormous magnitude. If we have been granted the luxury of being "normal," and unconsciously value "normal," making this adjustment is nearly impossible to describe. For me at the time it provoked feelings of rage, helplessness, frustration, resentment, a notable indifference to the larger issues that had before summoned me, and shame. The psychological impacts of what was happening to my body were such as to draw me deeply into myself, which under the circumstances was not a fun place to be. You can get a sense of some of this from the great writer James Jones, who noted that even the heroically wounded in combat were filled with shame at having been injured. Their anguish was over "being a drag and weight on their outfit." Jones comments, "Nor do the wounded seem to be less isolated from each other. Being in the same fix does not make them closer, but even further apart than they are from the well."[2] Part of the problem here is the internalization of stigma, the discriminatory prejudice we possess, usually unconsciously, toward the ill; here it is expressed against the self, which is dangerously close to home. The assaults upon the body, by themselves, almost seem unimportant when contrasted to the gigantic struggles that now begin to go on inside the self.

Racial minority people, oppressed women, gay men, lesbians, immigrants, people with disabilities of any sort, poor people have all had to come to terms with this inner struggle, forced by the social dimensions of our identity. And even among some of them the psychological burdens of illness add tragically to their suffering. I saw this vividly when in 1977, as a protective-services employee of the state, I took custody of a ten-year-old African-American child from a Jehovah's Witness family in Virginia. You may be aware that Jehovah's Witnesses are opposed to blood transfusions on religious grounds, even to save a life. The courts have regularly upheld the right of adults to refuse transfusions for themselves, but they have authorized state custody of Witness children for the purpose of obtaining life-saving transfusions for them. The little girl had been rushed to a major regional medical center after a rural physician had performed an emergency appendectomy. His clumsiness had led to peritonitis (a very dangerous infection of the peritoneum) and numerous perforations in the child's small intestine. Emergency life-saving surgery was performed upon her in the medical center emergency room; I then became involved as her custodian, to authorize further transfusions and surgical procedures that might be necessary.

As the long months of her hospitalization continued, and as I got to know her relatives better, I became aware of what she came to represent to them. Jehovah's Witnesses can look upon a child like this as a rape victim—someone upon whom a physical battery was performed against the person's will. I despaired over the family's view of this child and, even more, over her own perception of herself. As a rape victim she was "damaged goods." Her illness changed her identity fundamentally; it changed the way she was treated; it changed the way she was regarded by her family, by the community, and by herself.

The theological/philosophical writer who has addressed most poignantly the way illness attacks identity is Simone Weil. In an unforgettable essay entitled "The Love of God and Affliction," she talks about the self-loathing that the afflicted experience. They can damage even their own souls. The soul, she says, in its immense suffering, experiences *malheur*, which "stamps the soul to its very depths with . . . scorn and disgust."[3] Simone Weil believed we wreak this destruction by our attitudes, by our inability to appropriate our own God-given worth, by not doing or being able to do the one thing necessary in illness, which is to attend actively to the good. Such "attention" is our determined openness to God's saving grace.

A number of writers have covered this terrain with less religious terminology; they have arrived at similar insights. Cheri Register, for instance, suffers from a chronic liver disease. She writes from her experience of the trite reassurances that do not meet the case: "God never gives you more than you can handle," being one which rings false to her. She does concede, though, that "lived fully, the experience of illness can free you from the curse of perfectionism that makes happiness conditional on having everything just right." And another thought: "Through the gift of compassion [learned through one's own suffering], the experience of chronic illness offers protection against apathy, an indifference toward life that means, literally, 'not suffering.'"[4] As a chronically ill person, you learn in ways you never expected—never want others to have to learn—that at its very depths, life is struggle. There can be no apathy (not suffering), no escape from the constancy of the fight except temporarily in sleep.

Coming to terms with the never-endingness of all these things and the battle to cope itself can take its toll over the long haul. One tires. Maybe there was a time when the struggle was, at least in a strange way, interesting; but that time is now long gone. When there is no escape, another question may arise. This is treated in the splendid article by Stephen Schmidt in a May 3, 1989, issue of *The Christian Century* entitled "Living with Chronic Illness: Why Should I Go On?" Schmidt has lived with an awful disease, Crohn's syndrome, for twelve years, and he opens with this: "Everyone who lives with a long-term illness thinks about suicide at some time during that illness." But the desire to live is powerful, he says, and "courage faces the misery, faces death, faces despair, and still seeks to live."[5] He adds that a reason to want to live is out of consideration for other people with whom our lives are intertwined. (Since there is no other explanation for why the disease process that threatened my life all those years ago subsequently "burned out," I am left with my own view: One day it became blazingly clear to me that our kids were not going to grow up without their father. In this may be many different psychological dynamics, of course, but the *prima facie* matter of commitment to one's children, so far as I am concerned, is the operative one.)

PSYCHOLOGICAL AND SPIRITUAL EFFECTS OF ILLNESS

When illness comes upon someone, and the struggles which I have mentioned begin to take place, an opportunity arises for a change in one's life's direction, morally and spiritually speaking. This was best illustrated for me by one of Walker Percy's books, which presents a man who had a heart attack. When he began to recover in his hospital room, he stared at his hand, looked at it as if he had never seen it before; he was discovering it for the first time. With serious illness we can see things we never saw before. The same point is made in a short story called "The City" in John Updike's collection, *Trust Me*. In the story a man finds himself in a city that would seem ugly to most of us, but he suddenly requires emergency surgery. Thereafter, in convalescence, he sees something new, a lovely world:

> The drab housing and assembled rubble that he saw through the grid of the cement barrier, which permitted no broader view, nevertheless seemed to Carson brilliantly real, moist and deeptoned and full. Life, this was life. This was the world. When—still unable to climb stairs, the I.V. pole at his side—he had first come to this landing, just shoving open the door had been an effort. The raw outdoor air had raked through his still-drugged system like a sweeping rough kiss, early-fall air mixing summer and winter, football and baseball, stiff with chill yet damp and not quite purged of growth. Once, he heard the distant agitation of a lawnmower. Until the morning when he was released, he would come here even in the dark and lean his forehead against the cement and breathe, trying to take again into himself the miracle of the world, reprogramming himself, as it were, to live.[6]

At a moment like this a person can go through a sort of spiritual reorientation, and possibly a moral change. The late Mr. Lee Atwater, formerly the chair of the Republican party, gives us an example of this. Some time after he was diagnosed with a fatal brain tumor he apologized to a Columbia, South Carolina, politician for a callous and disparaging remark made concerning his earlier medical history. Atwater also apologized to Governor Dukakis for campaign "dirty tricks" practiced against him. (We all know, of course, that the various elements of sleaze politics are not confined to one political party). The religious term for a turnabout like this, anyway, is repentance. All of us know people who came to their better selves after the onset of illness.

The opportunities presented to Christian ministry in contexts like these are to help people ground their new story in the old, and the entire narrative within the larger story of God's grace. The great humanist physician Oliver Sacks said in an interview with Jonathan Cott, "Not only has every person with an illness or injury a story, and . . . not only are these stories interesting and varied, but . . . they also often have a quality of myth, of fairy tale, of dream. What interests me is the intersection between fact and fable. And in what appear to be the bleak rooms of clinics and chronic hospitals, I hear sagas, I see victims, I observe heroes, I witness great strivings of the human spirit."[7] The larger coherence of these strivings, and the stories that contain them, can be the story of redemption and trust in God.

Part of the story of the ill person is the experience of isolation. I have a dear friend whose daughter, now twenty-four, has been totally deaf from birth. The young woman attended a Christmas Eve service, but as she and her siblings and parents left the church she burst into tears. She conveyed her grief to her mother, saying that she was so sorry she would never hear her family's voices. She will never hear anyone's voice nor a Christmas carol. Her congenital hearing disability isolates her from the auditory things that connect us, draw us closer to mutual understanding, because words and music are experiences we all share. When I was told of this incident I thought of the justice predicates of the resurrection story, and of the last words of Beethoven, who never heard several of his own compositions: "I shall hear in heaven."

Whether caused by illness or physical disability, isolation can make you very vulnerable to other people. The *International Chris-*

tian Digest contained a poignant illustration of this when it quoted from a newsletter of Old Cutler Presbyterian Church in Miami, Florida. The pastor there was a man named Bob Davis. He had been an All-American football player and now was diagnosed with Alzheimer's disease. He wrote to his congregation, "The greatest fear I have is what this disease does to your personality. It can make you angry, ugly, obscene, paranoid, cursing, and very difficult to handle before you become comatose. Pray that I be spared part of this personality change. Pray that I in no way inadvertently disgrace the Lord, this church, or the people whom I love. Pray for Betty [my wife] as I turn guardianship over to her. I will not suffer nearly as much as she will. And please have patience with me. . . . Please remember me the way I was." We care about what others think of us, and when illness or disability makes us different from them, isolates us in some degree, we must count on their understanding and perhaps their mercy. This places great demands upon our spirits and perhaps theirs.

Being dependent upon others can be more stultifying than we want to admit—for us and for them. If that dependence shifts, however, even momentarily, we can feel liberation as a spectacular event, even as this provides the foil reminding us again of our predicament. I think now of the famous jazz pianist George Shearing. Shearing had been blind since his birth, and one day during a busy rush hour he waited at a crowded intersection to be taken across the street. Another blind person touched him and asked if he wouldn't mind helping him across the street. "What could I do?" said Shearing afterward. "I took him across and it was the biggest thrill of my life."[8]

In addition to isolation, the necessary downward adjustment of one's expectations brings considerable pressure upon the spirit. Some way of affirming one's predicament, and life, needs to be found. Success in this difficult task requires enormous courage. The Apostle Paul states, for instance, in II Corinthians 12:8, that "three times" he begged God to remove his handicap from him. God wouldn't cooperate, evidently, so Paul had to reconcile himself to the notion that his malady—whatever it was— served the positive purpose of preventing his self-glorification. Commenting on the II Corinthians passage, Krister Stendahl writes that "this insight, won through prayer, becomes a key to [Paul's] whole theology. Here in the very prayer life of Paul is the root of his famous theology of the cross." Stendahl cites II Corinthians 13:4 where Paul grounds his own experience in the story of Christ: "True, he died on the cross in weakness, but he lives by the power of God; and we who share his weakness shall by the power of God live with him in your service."[9]

I offer two further examples of diminished expectations and the positive adjustment of self in an affirming way. Each of these, I believe, shows what might be called, from a Christian perspective, the operations of God's grace to fortify courage. The first comes from *Plaintext*, by Nancy Mairs, a sufferer with multiple sclerosis:

> I can no longer walk very far from the armchair in which I read. I'll never make it to Tibet. Maybe not even to Albuquerque. Some days I don't even make it to the back yard. And yet I'm unwilling to forgo the adventuresome life: the difficulty of it, even the pain, the suspense and fear, and the sudden brief lift of spirit that graces—unexpectedly, inexplicably—the pilgrimage. If I am to have it too, then I must change the terms by which it is lived. And so I do. I refine adventure, make it smaller and smaller, until it fits into this little toad that struggles through the jungle of clover under my bare feet. And now, whether I am feeding fish flakes to my bettas or crawling across the dining room helping Burton look for his blind snake, lying wide-eyed in the dark battling yet another bout of depression, cooking a chicken, gathering flowers from the garden at the Farm, meeting a friend for lunch at the Blue Willow, I am always having the adventures that are mine to have.[10]

There is nothing glib here, but there is something heroic.

The second illustration of what I would call grace and courage and affirmation, despite the limitation imposed upon one's expectations, is from a book I found deeply moving and very beautifully written; it is by an anthropology professor paralyzed by a tumor on his spine:

> I was badly damaged, yet just as alive as ever, and I had to make the best of it with my remaining capabilities. It then occurred to me that this is the universal human condition. We all have to muddle through life within our limitations, and while I had certain physical handicaps, I retained many strengths. My brain was the only part of the central cortex that still worked well, but that also is where I made my living. "Disability" is an amorphous and relativistic term. Some people are unable to do what I do because they lack the mental equipment, and in this sense, they

are disabled and I am not. Everybody is disabled in one way or another. And even though my growing paralysis would one day end my active participation in the affairs of the world, I could still sit back and watch them unfold.[11]

Insights such as these, and the grace which infuses them, may be a long time coming, if they come at all. (We know people whose illness or disability has poisoned their spirits forever.) But whether individual cases reflect affirmation or despair, a Christian might begin with the surface meaning of stories like these, then understand them in deeper terms, as Paul did with his own disability. The more obscure meanings of life and its uncertainties may even surface, with the God question, in a fresh way; if so, then the ethics and spirituality issues may become more exigent for us too.

Afflicted people, real flesh-and-blood individuals, including Paul himself—if we will think of him as an ill person—may have much to teach us of the ways in which physical limitation can be the occasion of spiritual and moral growth. Here are stories of grace and beauty and, well, witness. And as the unique and precious individuals they are in our midst, disabled and chronically ill people are constant reminders of the human faces and human stories underneath the abstractions and generalizations of public policy. When we think of leadership in the area of health policy, then, as Christians we should think first not of economics or access or illness clusters or epidemiological findings or social priorities; we should instead think first of *this one* unique human being struggling in her or his soul to affirm life. For the Christian proclamation insists that abstracted aggregations are not our primary reference point, but individuals are. That is why the good shepherd went after the one and brought her back. Every one is infinitely valuable, because every one is infinitely loved by God.

STIGMA

Some believe that a popular children's nursery rhyme originated in the horrors of the great plague of medieval times. Consider this, which most children of my generation learned at an early age: "Ring-a-ring o' roses, / A pocket full of posies, / Ashes! Ashes! / We all fall down." A current theory holds that the ring-a-ring roses may describe the red rashes appearing on the bodies of plague victims. The pocket of posies might refer to the spices used to mask the odor of death in the community. "Ashes" is a corruption of the A-choo sound, signifying sneezing fits; and "we all fall down" needs no explanation. But the plague at least was indiscriminate. Although the sick were ominous signs to the healthy that the plague was too close at hand, plague victims were evidently not stigmatized by others in the community.

But others among the ill or disabled seem to have been singled out to suffer particular shame. The heartbreaking, but heartwarming, story of Joseph Carey Merrick, known as "the Elephant Man," displays the shame aspect of physical deformity. Merrick was born in Leicester, England, in 1862. He suffered with a disease known as multiple neurofibromatosis. The tissue beneath his skin in various places could be grasped in folds, so loose was the skin. Several growths of cauliflower texture appeared on his body. His right arm was twice or three times the size of the left. His head was massive and grossly distorted by tumorous growths. The shame he felt during his life, and the degradation to which he was subjected, was matched in its extremity only by the gentleness and beauty of his spirit. After he was befriended and protected by Dr. Treves of London Hospital, Merrick became well read in the English prayer book and Bible. He was eventually confirmed in the Church of England.

Merrick's physician, recognizing that his illness was incurable, had attempted at least to mitigate his loneliness. This, to me, is an affecting part of the story. The physician's kindness was efficacious, and Dr. Treves later wrote of his patient, "As a specimen of humanity, Merrick was ignoble and repulsive; but the spirit of Merrick, if it could be seen in the form of the living, would assume the figure of an upstanding and heroic man, smooth browed and clean of limb, and with eyes that flashed undaunted courage."[12] Joseph Merrick's final conversation with the chaplain of London Hospital contained an expression of his gratitude for the hospital, the people who had become his friends there, and for God who had led him to that place. Merrick's well-known largeness of spirit, and his crediting God and people like Treves, seem so poignant because of the shame and stigma that had to be dealt with in the first place.

The shame Merrick felt during most of his life is the same that people today must confront who are among the one in 400 born with facial deformities. Not all these people, or their families, can afford the plastic surgery needed to repair their features. Even today marriages come apart because of these deformities, and the deformed victims disproportionately get night jobs so they won't be seen by others; if they go to school they are frequently treated as if they were mentally retarded.[13] If I were a political leader I would fight for legislation enabling adults and children with severe facial deformities to be treated whether or not they had the money.

People with major deformities or physical features that set them apart are at serious risk for resentment—from others and from themselves. Folk musician Woody Guthrie, for instance, inherited a terrible illness from his mother; it rendered both of them increasingly disabled. The disease, Huntington's chorea, is described in Guthrie's wonderful book, *Bound for Glory*. In it he speaks of his mother: "She would be all right for a time and treat us as good as any other mother. And, all at once, it would start in—something bad and awful—something would come over her, and it came by slow degrees. Her face would twitch and her lips would snarl and her teeth would show . . . and she would double over into a terrible-looking hunch and turn into another person."[14]

When Woody himself developed symptoms of the same illness, rumors spread about its cause. On one occasion, "Woody nearly went berserk when he overheard a kid saying he was dying of syphilis. Slurred and blathering, he grabbed the kid and tried to explain that it wasn't syphilis, it was Huntington's chorea. HUNTINGTON'S CHOREA that came from his mother, and not from sleeping with whores or living out on the road. There was nothing, NOTHING he could have done about it. Nothing."[15] The disease hit Guthrie around the age of thirty. For the next fourteen years he became increasingly disabled and deranged, spending nearly all this time in a hospital. In his final three years he was hardly able to move or even speak. We have difficulty imagining the waves of resentment that well up inside someone with an illness like that, and threaten to disable the soul as completely as the body.

ILLNESS AND SOCIETY

I want to shift the focus now from the individual level to the social. My idea is that, having a more-or-less clear idea of the spiritual devastation that can be wrought upon individuals by illness or disability, Christians should now be in the appropriate posture to evaluate, and advocate for, effective health-care policy. I believe too that a morally healthy society is one in which all people have a chance for decent health care, and that as people concerned with love, justice, caring, fairness, and mutual regard, Christians should deeply be involved in the gigantic struggles presently going on in the public arena around health policy.

Environmental factors are part of the story. Ever since Lewis Carroll gave us the Mad Hatter, we should have been cognizant of the way an unhealthy environment may predispose the ill health of people in it. People in the hat-making trade used to display bizarre behavior, which apparently resulted from chronic poisoning due to the inhalation of mercury fumes in felt manufacturing. Today we don't need to go to the hat industry to find toxic fumes. They are as close, for instance, as the "smoking" section of your favorite restaurant—though the tobacco problem is by no means the only environmental health issue. Leon Howell, anyway, the talented editor of *Christianity and Crisis,* calls tobacco "our single biggest health problem." He quotes the American Cancer Society as predicting over 300,000 deaths from smoking-related diseases—over six times the number of deaths due to automobile accidents. We are ten times more likely to die of lung cancer if we smoke than if we don't. Your likelihood of dying from heart disease is twice as great if you are a smoker than if you are not. I could give you many more statistics, but I'm sure you get the idea.

But we should all be outraged at the way race is a factor in morbidity and mortality statistics. African-Americans now "suffer the highest rates of coronary heart disease and lung cancer of any population group."[16] Cigarettes are by far "the most heavily advertised product in America. . . . With nearly $3 billion in annual advertising, cigarettes are promoted twice as much as automobiles or alcohol, the next most advertised products." The well-known billboarding of racial minority and low-income areas by cigarette companies should be a matter of the deepest concern to all of us. Trading tobacco revenues for the bodies of our poor and racially oppressed is a cynical and scurrilous moral blight on our land.

The special health needs of vulnerable people require our most caring response. I went with a family nurse practitioner to visit the one city-operated shelter for homeless families in San Francisco. I learned there about the terribly difficult problems homeless people have in managing chronic illness. Consider diabetes, for instance. When you have to be out of a shelter early in the morning, and cannot reenter it until supper time, where do you go to inject insulin? What do you do when an addict steals your syringes? Where do you go to test your urine, and where do you take the results if they are problematic? Since a diabetic must be scrupulously time-conscious about monitoring his or her blood-sugar levels, and about taking insulin, the well-known loss of a time sense among the homeless is a devastating problem. A diabetic must control diet. But the homeless frequently eat whatever can be scrounged from dumpsters. The problems go on and on. The costs of treating a diabetic in crisis can be enormous—not to mention that having things get to the crisis state is not humane in the first place.

Whether one is diabetic or not, the morbidity and mortality rates among the homeless are heartbreaking. They soar especially in January. As the coldest month, it is the time of highest deaths due to hypothermia, exposure to the cold. From 1967 to 1987 deaths from excessive cold doubled in the U.S., from 327 to 631. Most of these deaths are those of older men, many of them alcoholics.[17] A physician attending at Harlem Hospital told me of the disturbing rise in TB cases treated there—treated in the face of a discouraging lack of ultraviolet-lighted and adequately ventilated rooms, and lack of computers necessary to track, city-wide, the medical records and treatment histories of wandering homeless people. Most of these immensely frustrating problems are avoidable, or would be, if our country willed itself to care for the homeless, which we could do but don't will to do enough.

There are some *with* housing, however, whose illnesses and mortality seem to depend upon where they live. Inner-city health problems are horrifying. A *New York Times* article on Christmas Eve, 1990, stated that "residents of the inner cities inhabit islands of illness, epidemics and premature death."[18] The problems are related to "new depths of urban poverty and inadequate medical services." The last four years especially have witnessed unprecedented increases in TB, hepatitis A, gonorrhea, measles, mumps, whooping cough, complex ear infections, and AIDS. A Los Angeles pediatrician reports that, "If you look at maps of measles outbreaks in Los Angeles and where the poverty is, they are the same."[19] The consequences of untreated, or undertreated chronic illness are severe in the impoverished inner city. In 1988 in central Harlem, for example, death rates from diabetes-related causes were five times that of the wealthier parts of New York City. Other debilitating chronic diseases, like asthma and epilepsy, are frequently undiagnosed in the inner city and untreated. "Dr. Harold P. Freeman, chief of surgery at Harlem Hospital . . . caused a stir [in early 1990] when he reported in the *New England Journal of Medicine* that a black man in Harlem was less likely to reach 65 years of age than a man in Bangladesh. While violent crime is part of the problem . . . high rates of disease were the primary cause."[20]

"In many studies, scientists compare black and white rather than rich and poor to eke out information about health-care differentials, since it is easier to figure out race than salary from medical records and far more blacks than whites live in the inner city. But most experts say it is primarily poverty, not race, that raises the risk [of poor health]."[21] Poverty, low birth rate (with its attendant tendencies to retardation, seizures, blindness, deafness, learning disabilities, and heart problems), inadequate housing, exposure to household toxins (especially lead), poor sanitation, childhood asthma-inducing tobacco smoke mainly from the mother, anemia from poor diets . . . the list of inner-city health problems is depressing and infuriating. "The National Center for Health Statistics first started comparing black-white infant mortality in 1950, and the difference has never been greater than it is today, with black babies dying at twice the rate before their first birthday. While the life expectancy of whites rose to 75.6 years in 1987, that of blacks fell to 69.2."[22] Dr. Beatriz Arpayaglou, of the Newark Children's Health Project, summed all this up in the remark that "We're seeing scenes here straight out of underdeveloped countries."[23]

The causes of these disgraceful facts are known: plain old poverty and the absence of a humane health-care system for all the people of our still-wealthy country. The means to address poverty and lack of health care are known; what is lacking is the will to undertake the job and leadership animated by sincere compassion. To the churches, with our long tradition of healing ministry—evidenced, for instance, by the establishment of numerous hospices and hospitals down the centuries—the relative stagnation of concern in this area must appear as striking. More, in face of our accountability to Jesus and his ministry of compassion, aided by the compassionate and empowering Spirit of God, no less, all this must be seen as a scandal. The church's traditional ministry of healing must take on a profound moral commitment in judgment of our skewed national priorities, and we must assume a renewed advocacy for the vulnerable. Where is Christian leadership in this area?

HEALTH INSURANCE

Under the present system, health care is not affordable for an increasing number of people. In 1993, over 37 million had no health insurance. You can see its skyrocketing costs by studying what employers pay for their employees' health insurance. In 1990, for instance, "fully 26 percent of the average company's net earnings went for medical costs," according to a survey by the Foster Higgins consulting firm.[24] "Health care cost an average of $3,217 for each worker in 1990, an increase of 17.1 percent from 1989. . . . The costs at large companies, with at least 40,000 employees, were even higher: $3,999 an employee."

The rate of cost increase was less with health-maintenance organizations. But ordinary medical costs have escalated by 20 percent yearly, and at this rate are projected to be above $22,000 per employee by the year 2000.[25] There are economic problems here of immense proportions, yes; but there are inequities, vested interests, and political opportunism, which when combined together prevent a comprehensive and effective solution to the problem. What ominous bell tolls for the moral integrity of our nation when, with the single exception of South Africa, the U.S. is the only industrialized nation in the world with no basic health plan covering all its citizens? When we talk of healing in this debt-ridden but still immensely wealthy country we must talk about healing the society as a whole, so that all its people can have a reasonable chance to make their way ahead.

What are a few of the proposed solutions? A growing number of people want to require employers to provide employees with health insurance (over 60 percent of people without health insurance work or are among the families of employees). Many people seek an expansion of the Medicaid plan drastically shrunk during the Reagan years. (Medicaid covers now only 40 percent of the poor, a decrease from 63 percent in the mid-1970s.)[26] A number of national commissions are studying the possibility of expanding the federal system in ways that resemble the Canadian program of coverage for all. The

Canadian plan, incidentally, received the highest degree of support of any health plans in a Harris survey of ten industrialized countries: 56 percent of Canadians said their program works "pretty well," as opposed to 10 percent of Americans.[27] The federal budget deficit in our country makes it unlikely, however, that a significantly enhanced national scheme will become a reality in the near future, according to some, even though monies are found for weapons systems, floundering Savings and Loans Associations, etc., etc. We can, and we must, write letters, register voters, and be activists for a decent and humane society. We should ourselves become leaders in this field, whether or not we formally fill official leadership slots; there is much analysis, criticism, advocacy, and overseeing that needs to be done.

In these emergent days the attention of some is upon the presumed prospects of the "Clinton plan." But in the shorter run, many are turning away from the federal government, which has appeared unable and unwilling to respond sufficiently to the health needs of the nation's poor. The focus is falling now upon the individual states. The "Oregon plan" is being studied by many states as a way of "rationing" health services to all people covered by Medicaid; this includes the poor, of course, who would be covered for certain essential benefits. The plan entails the identification of specific treatments that would be covered and the designation of others that would not—as decided by representatives of the people of Oregon themselves. Rare, hopeless, and extremely expensive services would be sacrificed, rather than those which are common, relatively inexpensive, or offer some reasonable hope of remediation or recovery. Over 1,600 medical procedures have been ranked in order of priority by means of polls in Oregon, with their attendant costs; after their adoption by the state legislature the overall plan must be approved by the Medicaid payer, which is the federal administration. The idea is that at last a rational and coherent plan would then be in place, with a list of health-care interventions publicly known; Medicaid funds to the state would be allocated in accordance with the prioritized list until the funds are exhausted. Needless to say, the plan is controversial, but it is being studied carefully for possible application elsewhere in the country.[28]

As of early August 1992, however, the White House stated its reluctance to approve the Oregon plan because it allegedly discriminates against people with either physical or mental disabilities. If so, this would put the plan into conflict with the Americans with

Disabilities Act (ADA) of 1990—an act that I believe is an important sign of progress in our country, and which essentially holds that "no qualified individual with a disability shall, by reason of such disability, be excluded from participation in or be denied the benefits" of any public program.

This apparent conflict with Oregon's plan illustrates the difficulties of obtaining a just (fair, equal, inclusive) health-care plan—because of insufficient funding in the first place. Critics in Washington today say that because the prioritizing of Oregon health-care services was done in accordance with "quality-of-life" criteria, certain interventions with disabled people were assigned a low priority— due to the public view that a particular disability entails a low quality of life. This utilitarian approach means that when the limited funds have all been applied to higher-priority items, certain services to people with disabilities must be denied. But this denial is in violation of entitlements contained in the 1990 ADA. A question Oregon officials may now pose to the White House is whether or not every Medicaid program in the nation discriminates against the ADA, since no state presently extends unlimited Medicaid support to all disabled people. Unless and until there is a willingness to find more health-care funds (I'd suggest looking into the over $300 billion per year military budget), the debate will continue.

SOME PROPOSALS

I am taking the position that church leaders, and Christian leaders in society, ought to be as deeply, sincerely, and effectively concerned about the health of the public in our nation as we are concerned about the health of any individual in our parish or family. I could cite any number of biblical references in support of this, but I'll mention only one, the Good Samaritan parable, in which Jesus defines the neighbor as *any one* in need, like the one particular Jew who was in need and was taken care of by his presumed enemy, the Samaritan. With this as the essential predicate, I want to attend now to some further thoughts about our Christian response to the plight of ill people in our society.

My first suggestion is that we reexamine, then repent of, some of our previous attitudes concerning ill people. The prejudice against those physically or mentally different from us goes deep and, I believe, affects our willingness to respond to their needs. This prejudice has been blatant at times in our history, as in 1925, for instance, when the Episcopal Church's General Convention "reaffirmed its support for eugenics." The Joint Commission on Family Life submitted a eugenics report in that year opposing the marriage of people "deemed mentally unfit." This report was sent by the entire convention to all clergy. In 1927 the Episcopal Church by a "majority decision" expressed itself in favor of mandatory sterilization of retarded people to prevent their reproduction.[29]

These kinds of actions suggest a difficulty, at least at that time, in relating compassionately and respectfully to a vulnerable sector of society—people whose disability makes them different from us. This brings to mind the "Five Rules of the World," attributed to the Jesuit Tom Weston, and told to me by a friend. They go roughly like this: One, you must have nothing wrong with you; two, if you do, you must get over it immediately; three, if you can't get over it, pretend you did; four, if you can't even pretend, just don't show up, because it is too painful for the rest of us; and five, if you insist on showing up, you should at least have the decency to be ashamed. Mobilizing Christian leadership for positive action especially on behalf of today's impoverished ill, many of whom are a racial minority, requires a purging of a profoundly worrisome spiritual illness: the eugenics frame of mind, which is a view that people different from us shouldn't be around, or at least not around *us*.

A second suggestion is that Christian people and leaders understand and embody as fully as possible that (in the words of Leonard A. Sagan) "More important in explaining the decline in death worldwide is the rise of hope and the decline in despair and hopelessness."[30] To be able to be hopeful, and thus presumably more disposed to health, means having access to education, a strong sense of support and community, and the assurance that basic needs will be provided for. Dr. Sagan believes that hopelessness and helplessness set us up for bad health, and that these are demonstrably connected to socioeconomic status; his fine book documents this in the U.S. and elsewhere around the world. Church people, who at least in some degree understand the healing, affirmative, nurturing spirit of God, could easily make the application of this spiritual insight to the physical conditions that affect bodily health. There is room for a large teaching and servant ministry here in every parish, and there are enormous implications for Christians in formal or informal leadership roles in society.

A third suggestion is that churches be centers of knowledge, support, and advocacy, where the things associated with physical, mental, and spiritual health are openly discussed and where people may mobilize themselves for their own health and the health of others. At the least, clergy and lay leaders should become familiar with the major health aspects of people's lives. Seminary courses and/or continuing-education programs should be designed to delve into such health matters as chronic illness (physical and emotional aspects of the same), the aging process, basic medical and nursing terminology, the special problems of people with disabilities, and the like.

Educational forums in the parish should address issues ranging from the use of durable power of attorney for health care, to helping people place loved ones appropriately in health-care facilities, to addressing issues locally and regionally that bear upon illness-inducing toxic waste, to seeing to it that the poorest in their community have equal access to the health providers there. Because of the movement in clinical pastoral education many seminary graduates are fluent in the things that belong to so-called mental illnesses; we need to become fluent, and active, in the things of physical well-being too.

A fourth suggestion is that Christian leaders, in the church and out, create an environment, with borders as far reaching as possible, within which the stigma of illness or disability is simply not allowed. I refer to countercultural zones of freedom, like that which the Southern Baptist preacher created when he put his arms around the man horribly crippled, wept with him, and spoke the words of the Baptist hymn to him, "I can almost see heaven from here"— pointing to a promise to all of us that some day we will be free of the limitations of the body and of the insecurity and perhaps even the shame that came upon us when we discovered we were not like the healthy or the beautiful people. And, by the same promise, we shall also be liberated from perhaps our own bigotry and fear concerning ill and disabled people who threaten us.

I cannot fail to emphasize again the Christian accent upon the value of each one, especially in a social context of ignorance and fear. I clipped an article from a *Harper's* magazine once that contained an essay for a workshop in autobiography at Columbia University. It was called "AIDS Stories" by a man named John Weir, and it contained this:

> The last memorial service I attended for a member of the group was Gerald's. He died the day of the last workshop. He had been in the group from the beginning, even before I started running it. He was an intern in radiology at a hospital on the East Side when he was diagnosed. For about a year he looked perfectly healthy. Then he came back early from a vacation in Atlanta and went straight into the hospital. His lesions multiplied and he went on chemotherapy. When I first met him, Gerald was a dandy— fastidiously dressed, charming, affable. He wore wonderful argyle socks and a big ring with his initials on it; he flirted with everyone. But he fell apart very quickly. He lost a lot of weight and his hair fell out. A month after he was admitted to the hospital, he died. He was twenty-eight.
>
> His memorial service was at the Gay Synagogue in the Village. Gerald had a big, supportive, family. They all knew he was gay. The service was in Hebrew. His father got up to read his part. Gerald's father was the kind of Jewish man that Bernard Malamud wrote about—barely assimilated, still with the rough edges, the accent, the conspicuousness of an immigrant. He was a butcher in the Bronx.
>
> He started reading, but then he let go of the text, and tipped his head back, and clasped his palms together, and roared. He wailed and shouted and roared in a language that I couldn't understand, but I knew exactly what he meant. I knew exactly what he meant. I think I knew exactly what he meant.

The young man Gerald could be anyone's son. Church people must understand and present the most stigma-laden situations as stories of human suffering—suffering that the most bigoted person can relate to.

My next suggestion is that, either by their own experience of suffering or perhaps by their ability to imagine it, Christians should open the borders of their community to invite in those named in what Albert Schweitzer called "the Fellowship of those who bear the Mark of Pain. Who are the members of this Fellowship? [he asked.] Those who have learned by experience what physical pain and bodily anguish mean, belong together all the world over; they are united by a secret bond. One and all, they know the horrors of suffering to which [people] can be exposed, and one and all they know the longing to be free of pain." When a Christian community invites these kinds of people in, it all the more embodies the ultimate inclusiveness we have with God in God's Kingdom. We begin to realize the unique community we are, distinct from the normalizing, and thus excluding, tendencies of the larger society.

CARITAS

It has been my privilege to teach as a clinical faculty member at the University of California Health Sciences Campus in San Francisco. In that capacity I have met with a master's-degree class of pediatric nurses and participated in a discussion on informed consent. We listened as one of them told of a thirteen-year-old-boy with a form of bone cancer known as osteogenic sarcoma. The doctors advised his parents that to save his life they would have to amputate not only the boy's arm but also a large portion of his clavicle, and indeed a good chunk of his upper left quadrant. The parents, who were "model parents," in the words of the nurse, worked carefully to prepare the child for the operation. (Recall how much your body image mattered to you at age thirteen.) After the surgery the boy awoke in the hospital. He stared at where his arm and shoulder had been. He shrieked, "They took it!" and "I didn't know." When the boy tried to sit up in bed, he fell to the right side, his body mass not being balanced any more. The nurse started to cry as she explained to us, "There was nothing I could do. Just lie on his bed with him, hold him, and cry with him." I think this story serves as an unself-conscious example of the sincerity and compassion that Jesus wanted from us.

Stories like this pose the big theological questions of suffering. We don't know the solutions to these large mysteries, or even the small ones. But daily we are given opportunities to respond to the needs of the ill. In our response is the clue to what we really do believe in. Maybe if we undertake the caring action, the insights will follow—at both the level of ministry to individuals and in the public forum, where insistently compassionate leadership is so vitally important.

Christian people, and especially influential leaders, should work for the development of human and financial resources, religious or not, to ease the psychological or spiritual transition of some of us from being healthy to being ill people; it is not for nothing that in our society "the bottom line" refers to money. The financial resources, once fought for and obtained, should be used to deal with the enervating fatigue of battling illness and disability constantly. It should be used to help people with the shock of being dependent, and all the other things that go with not being any longer the persons we thought we were. Many Christians have a bizarre aversion even to discussing money; but without a tough-minded determination to get it and guarantee its rightful allocation, the sincerity of any discussion of health needs is seriously at risk of seeming fatuous.

At the social level, competent, tenacious leadership is needed to educate the wider community in such a way as to increase understanding, while diminishing shame-induced stigma associated with illness or disability; tobacco and a multitude of other environmental pathogens should more effectively be controlled throughout our country, by public policy; health care should be delivered more aggressively and effectively to homeless people and others disadvantaged; a major new start needs to be made at all levels ranging from education to aggressive service delivery in the rotting cores of our inner cities—for health-care matters ranging from maternal and infant nutrition to AIDS prevention and treatment. There must be health insurance for all in this still rich country, for justice requires no less.

Leadership advocacy for the health care of all is today's way of continuing the honorable tradition of Christian healing. To care about the wellness of people we'll never meet can seem very Quixotic indeed in a world filled with self-serving. But it was Quixote himself who showed us the way of faith in these matters. In days of yore, some used to believe in the "balsam of Fierabras," a wonderful healing unguent that embalmed Christ's body, according to the legend. This balsam had been carried away by Fierabras, a heroic knight in Charlemagne's court. One drop of it would heal any sickness or overcome any wound instantly. In his wonderful, childlike enthusiasm, Don Quixote proclaims to his comrade, "It is the balsam of balsams; it not only heals all wounds, but even defies death itself. If thou should'st see my body cut in two, friend Sancho, by some unlucky backstroke, you must carefully pick up that half of me which falls to the ground, and clap it upon the other half before the blood congeals, then give me a draught of the balsam of Fierabras, and you will presently see me sound as an orange." (I.ii.2 of *Don Quixote*)

All people, but especially the Christians among us, should care sincerely about *all* the ill people of this world and dream the impossible dream of a world based on the sweetness and caring of Jesus, a world of justice—where each person counts the same. This is simply and exactly what we are called to as Christians. *This is the one thing needful* to make us all *spiritually* sound as an orange. Too many people have suffered too needlessly and too much. If Quixote was a madman, we should all be mad like him.

DISCUSSION QUESTIONS

1. What is your experience of the psychological or spiritual implications of illness?
2. Do you believe it is more difficult for a person of color than for a Caucasian to receive quality health care in our country?
3. What effect, if any, does poverty have on gaining access to health services?
4. Do you think the sale of tobacco products to anyone should be banned in our country?
5. Should smokers pay at significantly higher health insurance rates than nonsmokers?
6. Should there be a national policy mandating housing for everyone with chronic illness?
7. What are the impediments to universal health insurance in the U.S.?
8. Does caring ministry to an ill individual imply an equal commitment to changing health policy for all?

THE CHURCH AND
THE PLIGHT OF CHILDREN

This is an ancient midrash: "When Israel stood to receive the
Torah, the Holy One, blessed be He, said to them: I am giving
you my Torah. Bring me good guarantors that you will guard
it, and I shall give it to you. They said: Our fathers are our guarantors. The Holy One, blessed be He, said to them: Your fathers are
unacceptable to me. Bring me good guarantors, and I shall give it
to you. They said to him: Master of the Universe, our prophets are
our guarantors. He said to them: Your prophets are unacceptable to
me. Yet bring me good guarantors, and I shall give it to you. Behold,
our children are our guarantors. The Holy One, blessed be He,
said: They are certainly good guarantors. For their sake, I give you
the Torah."[1]

The prospects of children are directly dependent upon the concern or the neglect of our highest officials. I am going to hound and
harass you for a few minutes with some grim facts and statistics
about children, such as that in 1970 the Joint Commission on the
Mental Health of Children reported that more children under the
age of five in our country are killed each year by their parents than
die from disease. And that today, "Every 53 minutes an American
child *dies* because of [plain old] poverty."[2] But first I'd like to tell you
about a twelve-year-old child whom I met one day when I worked as
a state investigator of child abuse and child neglect. I'd like to tell
you about her briefly, because I think you could see in her both the
moral grandeur of her life and also the terrible burden she bears.

Irene is twelve years old, comes from a deprived home, as it is
said. Her dad is in his early sixties; he was born in "the [Caribbean]
islands" and worked in Panama as a young man. Usually he worked
in agriculture, oil-field drilling, and did whatever else he could find.

Irene's mama does not function well as a parent. She can't keep the roaches off the walls of the tiny home they rent. She can't keep the children's clothes clean. She can't get to school for a meeting with the teacher, nor can she get the kids to the doctor. She can't keep peace in her home among the seven children. Mother is ineffectual, passive, disorganized, inept. Irene tries to help her mother run the house.

Father is gone most of the time, but when he is home, he is very demanding. Mama keeps a pot of water boiling on the stove all the time; a neighbor says it's there to be used against her husband if he becomes abusive.

I visit Irene's school, where her teacher says, "Irene smells so bad when she comes to school that other children push her out of her seat on the bus. Her clothes are messy, her sneakers are ripped open in the front—no matter whether it's summer or winter. She appears not to care how the other children feel toward her."

When we meet, I look into a twelve-year-old face. Does she appear to be an older woman, or do I only imagine it? She composes herself and looks into the distance. She talks matter-of-factly, without self-pity. "They worry me when they get in fights. I can whip most of the children they fight with, but sometimes I know I can't. I have to just keep them home and hope no trouble follows them to our house. The children [referring to the younger siblings] they're afraid of their mama cause she'll whip them with a belt; but they're not afraid of me. I won't touch them except to pick them up. Sometimes there's enough to eat, sometimes there isn't. I don't know what happened last night. I just didn't eat. Yes, I think there was some food in the house. I just didn't eat. I don't know why."

Her brown eyes scan the school yard. I ask her how she feels about having to take so much responsibility for the children. She shows no self-pity. Matter-of-factly she repeats, "I worry about their fights in the neighborhood." And now she looks down toward her torn tennis shoes. Her hands are behind her back. She is beginning to develop breasts. She leans on a railing; her blouse is held together with buttons and a large safety pin near the top. I am so deeply moved by this child. I find her courage, her humanity, so, well, sacred is the only word for it. But the sadness about all this is indescribable. It has to do with her not having had much of a childhood. These many years later I cannot get this child out of my mind. Whatever became of her? What becomes of others like her?

Harvard philosopher Hilary Putnam wrote of children like this when he identified the moral choices poor children make every day, without any audience to applaud them or commission to honor them. They could "do evil things—sell terrible drugs, run prostitution and gambling rackets, and even commit murders; but . . . also live comfortably . . . and perhaps enjoy a kind of respect and admiration." But sacrificing for the right and good may mean "a life of almost unimaginable poverty [and perhaps seeing] some of the children [they] will have to "undergo immense privation as well." Putnam writes, "Some of the bitterest sacrifices that people make for what is right are (and, indeed, must be) taken as simply a matter of course . . ."[3] There is a heroic morality at work here, the kind that seldom gets taught, or even recognized, in many institutions of higher education. Robert Coles describes it in *The Moral Life of Children*. He does not know its origin, nor do I. For religious people, however, or any of us, it is a phenomenon worth noting.

SOME HISTORICAL NOTES ON CHILDHOOD

It is possible that we can gain a better appreciation for the status of children today by looking a bit at the past.[4] The overall historical picture is bleak. In ancient Jericho, around 7000 B.C., children were sealed into a city wall to fortify its structure. In ancient Sparta, a council of elders exercised their responsibility to examine all newborns; if they appeared to be promising supporters of the military state, they were spared; if not, they could be destroyed. In Athens the life-or-death question was decided by the child's father; apparently his criterion tended to be whether the child was likely to be a burden to the family. Needless to say, most of the children destroyed, or left to die by the method of exposure, were the sick, the crippled, the illegitimate, and the females.

In the Bible you get what appears to be a touching indication of consideration for children in Genesis 33:13–14, where Jacob talks to his brother. Esau has proposed that the two of them, now apparently reconciled at last, travel together. Jacob says, "My lord knows that the children are frail, and that the flocks and herds nursing are a care to me . . . I will lead on slowly . . . according to the pace of the children." This is heartwarming until you remember that Jacob's main concern is not for the children, but for himself. He is possessed of an enormous guilty fear of his brother, of course, and the pace of the children becomes his excuse not to travel with the man he had wronged, whom he still cannot bring himself to trust. I can find no compelling evidence that children in ancient Israel were much regarded as intrinsically valuable creatures of God. Orphans, with widows, were a concern to the prophets; their rights in God, however, seem necessitated by the absence of any rights in society. What the Bible says throughout about children is better researched by someone other than me. The first recourse is the trusty *Interpreter's Dictionary of the Bible,* but the entry there for children is sparse.

The picture gets a little brighter for children in the New Testament—at least with Jesus. He rebuked people who tried to shield him from them, and said that theirs was the Kingdom of heaven. Also he apparently referred to children when he remarked that any who caused them to stumble would be better off with a giant millstone round his or her neck, drowning in the sea. On the other hand, St. Paul seems to have thought of childhood as largely irrelevant: "When I was a child I thought like a child . . . but when I became an adult I put away childish things." The picture for kids does not get brighter with Augustine. He evidently regarded children as "conceived in iniquity" and thus bad-tempered, sinfully egocentric, and the like.

By the twelfth century, Pope Innocent was appalled at the sight of "countless" infant bodies floating in the Tiber River. He encouraged the spread of foundling homes in Italy (the first foundling hospital had been established in Milan in A.D. 787). But the foundling hospitals throughout Europe frequently ended up selling infants to beggars, who would cripple them to evoke sympathy and alms; this is the historical origin of the familiar figure of the beggar child on a crutch.

Meantime, because the church was opposed to abortion, child abandonment became the preferred way to limit family size. A recent and acclaimed study by Yale historian John Boswell is fascinating on this subject. The problem was that an additional child burdened an already precarious food supply and space limitation in many families. The parents who abandoned newborns in places like monasteries, for instance, did so out of a sincere regard for the best interest of the child, according to Boswell. Florence is where the best documents can be found on child abandonment in the later Middle Ages. Here half of all abandoned children came from poverty, a third of them were the children of household slaves, perhaps impregnated by wealthy men, and over two-thirds were girls. The astonishing discovery Boswell claims to have made is that "at no point did European society as a whole entertain serious sanctions against the practice." The prevailing ethic apparently supported the practice of abandoning children, or ignored it. In the Roman world, the word for cast-off children fortunate enough to be taken in by rescuing foster parents, is *alumni*—referring to the dual role of foster child and pupil-servant. Conceivably Christian motivation could have been found on the part of the merciful foster parents. To quote Boswell, "Christians saw themselves as God's alumni, and, directly or by implication, Christian literature was filled with positive and idealized images of adoption and of transference from natural families to happier and more loving adopted kin groups, including such influential metaphors as the 'adoption' of the Gentiles, adoption into a monastic 'family' or baptism itself, the foundation of the Christian experience."5

I again skip over much historical material to get us closer now to home. In the U.S., in 1871, a nineteen-year-old girl named Mary Ellen was found chained to her bed in a seedy New York City apartment. The woman who found her, a public-health nurse, tried to obtain a court order to have the young woman unchained. There was no law on the books that would support this move, for Mary Ellen was legally a minor and therefore the property of the people who had shackled her. The nurse subsequently went to the SPCA, who succeeded in getting Mary Ellen freed on the legal ground that she was a member of the animal kingdom, and laws protecting animals did exist that could be applied to her situation. The case led some few years later to the first U.S. law protecting children.

Today anyone who reads the newspapers, never mind the reports of groups such as the Children's Defense Fund, the Center for the Study of Social Policy, and others, knows that the decade of the 1980s in this country was a disaster for children—especially for poor and racial-minority kids. The most succinct presentations of today's problems for kids are issued regularly by the Children's Defense Fund. For example, one in five U.S. kids—12 million—lives in poverty. One in five kids has no health insurance. The portion of our population most quickly becoming homeless are families with children. It is currently estimated that every day 135,000 kids in our country take a gun to school. ("Children are safer in Northern Ireland than in America," the Fund says.)

The *New York Times* in late January 1991 ran a three-piece series describing child poverty and other domestic problems in our country and noted that no initiative was being taken anywhere in the political arena to respond to them. The *Times*, in lamenting the absence of a concerted public effort to meet the needs of the poor, spoke of a "missing agenda." By March 17, 1991, the *Times* had come upon a dreadful effect of this social neglect. It reported that "nearly half of black male Americans from 15 to 19 years old who died in 1988 were killed by guns." The then Secretary of Health and Human Services, Dr. Louis W. Sullivan, was quoted as saying, "Do you realize that the leading killer of young black males is young black males?" He continued, "During every 100 hours on our streets, we lose more young men than were killed in 100 hours of ground war in the Persian Gulf. Where are the yellow ribbons of hope and remembrance for our youth dying in the streets? This is a war against ourselves, and it is devastating our communities."

What is a possible solution to all this that the churches might pursue? We could understand first that our nation's children are paying a terrible price for our misplaced national priorities. But our second thought is that when we send our own kids to an exclusive school, provide our own kids with well-furnished homes and the best doctors, but then vote for politicians and policies that blight the lives of poor children, we are practicing an oppressive role morality—in my role as a parent, I'm doing what's good only for MY kids.

Some will recognize parent role morality as a form of the proximity ethic known as NIMBY, "Not in my back yard," where the problems of others remain outside my immediate concern in practice. A Christian ethic would urge us to be as concerned about the children we don't know as we are about our own kids; it makes no room for privilege-based role morality. If we can get clear about the conceptual difference between role and common morality, we should be able to do much more in the churches to push for a common morality commitment to all people. We ought to recognize that what defeats such heroic little kids as Irene and those 12 million others in poverty is not just lousy parenting (for which the children themselves can hardly be held accountable, nor frequently their parents) but all too often miserly social programs, and ignorance-based neglect by social and political leaders of our country. The people who are killing the nation's children are they who are protecting their own *only*.

For a moment I'd like to expand the geopolitical scope of these remarks. On the larger world scene, some 40,000 children under the age of five die each day from malnutrition and disease.[6] The U.N. General Assembly on November 20, 1989, adopted the International Convention on the Rights of the Child. Several basic rights for children were set forth. Among these were the right to survival, education, and a name. Forbidden is their exploitation or forced removal from a parent. This convention promised to advance the prospects of millions of kids around the world. But the U.S. obstructed the drafting of this document by resisting a provision that would have set eighteen as the minimum age for military combat. The U.S. argued that the Geneva Convention already established the age of fifteen for this.[7] The reasoning was, if the earlier convention allows fifteen-year-old soldiers, why change it?

By late September 1990 the U.N. convened its World Summit for Children. Leaders from over seventy nations met—if not entirely out of consideration for the intrinsic value of kids, at least out of concern for them as a precious national resource—future producers, and all that. Goals were set for the year 2000: to reduce infant and child mortality by a third, to cut child malnutrition in half, to provide education and access to safe drinking water for all children, and to eradicate polio worldwide. Again, these were significant steps forward, promising a better prospect for sick kids, hungry kids, illiterate kids. But despite the lofty rhetoric, no nation has come forth with the money to enable the goals to be achieved. The delegates promoted the Convention on the Rights of the Child, which I mentioned a moment ago, and which had been worked on for ten years. Of the world's 160 nations 109 have by now signed this convention. The U.S. has not. Our current objection is that the convention would prohibit execution of anyone under the age of eighteen. (Only Iran, Bangladesh, Iraq, and the U.S. still execute juvenile offenders. This is not glorious company.)

Besides the intrinsic value of kids, there are economic reasons to plan for their long-range welfare. In the U.S., for instance, it costs $8.00 to inoculate a child with measles vaccine, but it costs $5,000 to care for a child with measles in a hospital. It costs $600 for nine months of prenatal care for a healthy pregnant woman, but over $2,500 per day to care for a hospitalized premature child.[8] Maternal and child health is the area where altruism and economic self-interest coincide: doing the right thing pays.

I shift gears here. I want to talk about the positive valuation of children, and I turn to some of the writers who express these things so well. I happen to think that James Agee was not only one of our best writers, but also one of our most kindly and passionately disposed advocates of children. In his famous book *Let Us Now Praise Famous Men* he wrote, "In every child who is born, under no matter what circumstance and no matter what parents, the potentiality of the human race is born again and in him, too, once more and of each of us, our terrific responsibility toward human life: toward the utmost idea of goodness, of the horror of terror, and of God."[9] Agee's splendid book presented the lives of poor dirt farmers and share-croppers in the deep South and the lives of their children. He saw in the kids the poignancy, the affirmation, and the courage that we'd like to find in ourselves.

And while we are considering a novelist, I want to mention a lovely phrase used by Don DeLillo for children in *White Noise*. He calls them "guardians of the heart." But thinking of Agee and DeLillo in these matters reminds me of still another writer, Ariel Dorfman. In *The Last Song of Manuel Sendara*, the children, while in utero, refuse to be born until the mess of the world is cleaned up by their parents. Bully for them.

WHAT ARE SOME CHARACTERISTICS
OF A JUST AND PEACEABLE SOCIETY
FRIENDLY TO CHILDREN?

Supposing that we were roused by the dire prospects for some of the world's kids, and that we were impelled to care for them, what sorts of objectives would we seek to meet?

1. The society we would pursue would have greatly reduced the violence in which children are raised. I think just now of our daughter, Amy, who taught twenty-six Puerto Rican kids in a bilingual classroom in Bedford-Stuyvesant, Brooklyn. When a seventh-grader at her school was shot to death one day, she encouraged her fifth-graders to talk about their concerns. She discovered to her horror and sorrow that each of them is trained to grab their younger siblings and push or pull them away from windows when shots are fired

nearby. All these families had discussed this strategy with these ten-year-old kids as a *matter of course*.

This is but one vignette related to the disturbing statistic recently reported by the Federal Centers for Disease Control that the homicide rate for African-American men from the ages of fifteen to twenty-four has risen by two-thirds in the FIVE years through 1988. Overwhelmingly this increase is positively correlated with the availability of handguns. The homicide rate is rising fastest for African-American males aged fifteen to nineteen. Dr. Robert Froehlke, the main author of the CDC report, was quoted as saying, "In some areas of the country it is no more likely for a black male between his 15th and 25th birthday to die from homicide than it was for a United States soldier to be killed on a tour of duty in Vietnam."[10]

But the problem is not only with handguns. Amy's roommate Kate taught seventh-graders. The kids at her school are organized in gangs according to their housing project. Kate's kids for some reason come from a project where no gang has yet been organized, so they regularly get jumped after school by bigger kids from a different housing project. One kid begged Kate to dismiss him early so that he could get home safely; he didn't want to get beat up any more. One day Kate let him go a few minutes early, but the principal caught the kid, disciplining him AND Kate. Of course the schools by themselves can't solve all society's problems. But the schools can't do much of anything to educate, either, if kids are worried about being beaten up, or if they come to school hungry, or if they have gotten no sleep the night before. The New York City schools, incidentally, had to cut $70 million dollars from their budgets that year. *Before* the cuts Amy had to buy paste and glue with her own money, and things to decorate her classroom. All this leads to the thought that the worst forms of violence may be battery with a handgun or knife; but whatever violates the spirit of a child is violence too, including the endless grinding poverty and the shabby schools with their chintzy budgets.

And of course there is the violence of verbal abuse that so frequently goes on in homes. I recognize it is terribly difficult to reach this problem and deal with it; but some of the perpetrators do go to our churches. It is disturbing to discuss violence at such length, but violence occurs partly because we who can ignore it find it agreeable to do so. Please indulge my last example of violence, which used to vex me terribly when I'd see it in my protective-services work.

I am thinking now of a police report that crossed my desk years ago when I worked in the protective-services business. The crime report form asks for the victim's race, sex, age, and weapon used. There is a section where the officer describes how the attack occurred. On this report concerning an eleven-year-old white male, under "weapon" the officer had put "mouth." In describing the attack he had written, "Parents directed continuous degrading remarks to and about the child/victim." This section concluded, "The entire time I was present they did not say anything nice about their son. The family environment is not conducive to the physical and mental growth of the child." (When I first read this report I wanted to meet the officer who had written it. He seemed a saint of God.) The shouting, screaming, hounding, belittling, ridiculing, and humiliation practiced against children must be stopped. The churches can play a major part in this.

2. The loneliness of children would be mitigated in a more humane society. A recent book by Richard Louv, entitled *Childhood's Future*,[11] documents the isolation of children from their parents and the disintegration that can occur in the quality of life for all. One child is quoted to this effect: "I never really knew my parents too well, or my grandparents or any of my relatives. . . . It's kind of like a separate world of mine." Not only is this a problem within the family; it is a problem within society's larger structures. Louv looks at the child-caring institutions that are supposed to buttress the child's life when he or she is left to them by parents, and these he finds underfunded, understaffed, sometimes bleak, and on and on. Louv places the responsibility for the loneliness of children not only upon their parents, but also upon a society that alone among the Western nations, he says, devalues family life and usually in fact makes it very difficult for a working parent to stay home with a newborn.

The paradigm for our money-worshipping society, and its adverse consequences for children, is a *New Yorker* cartoon that I once saw. In it a small girl holding a ball stands before a successful older man who is offering her some cash as he says, "I'm sorry, but I'm not very good with children. Here's twenty dollars." The children of affluence are at risk for emotional neglect. Emotionally they are in danger of becoming orphans, and I have seen them at my house daily. My son collects male companions, nearly all of whose parents are divorced, most of them with ample financial resources. If there were such a thing as "failure-to-thrive" adolescents, these would be they. Their loneliness is palpable, though they wouldn't admit it to a stranger. They remind me of this passage from Eileen Simpson, who wrote about orphans:

> Dickens chided readers of his newspaper articles for not visiting almshouses and orphanages to see how the inmates were being treated. In a country where until the early part of the nineteenth century the gentry had regarded a visit to Bedlam to see the insane as a Sunday's entertainment, it was self-protectiveness that kept them from responding to Dickens's prodding. Orphans provide no entertainment. They don't cry, scream, shout, or behave bizarrely. Instead they observe visitors in searching silence. It was an unwillingness to look into these eyes and to read their message, that kept people away. . . . For me, the children's eyes would have unspoken messages: You were more fortunate than we are, they would say. Or, more distressingly: Take us with you.[12]

Even under ideal social circumstances children can have an awful time with loneliness, as is brought out neatly in John Cheever's diary, which describes the loneliness we may have forgotten since our own adolescence: "And walking back from the river I remember the galling loneliness of my adolescence, from which I do not seem to have completely escaped. It is the sense of the voyeur, the lonely, lonely boy with no role in life but to peer in at the lighted windows of other people's contentment and vitality. It seems comical—farcical—that, having been treated so generously, I should be stuck with this image of a kid in the rain walking along the road shoulders of East Milton."[13]

Well, loneliness is a fixed part of life. It is there for all of us, and we have the responsibility to command our own lives in such a way as to minimize its dreadful effects. Sure. But I am saying that it is there in children, too, and we need to look for it if we are ever going to help them deal with it. And the churches are presumably the custodians of a message about a world, and a humanity, not alone, but loved by God, and quite importantly, loved by God's people.

3. Ours would be a world in which children were nurtured in their uniqueness. In *Joys and Sorrows*, Pablo Casals wrote, "Each

second we live in a new and unique moment of the universe, a moment that never was before and will never be again. And what do we teach our children in school? We teach them that two and two make four, and that Paris is the capital of France. When will we also teach them what they are? We should say to each of them: Do you know what you are? You are a marvel. You are unique. In all the world there is no other child like you. And look at your body—what a wonder it is! Your legs, your arms, your cunning fingers, the way you move! You may become a Shakespeare, a Michelangelo, a Beethoven. You have the capacity for anything. Yes, you are a marvel. And when you grow up, can you then harm another who is, like you, a marvel? You must cherish one another. You must work—we must all work—to make this world worthy of its children."

What Casals is after is so profoundly different from the achievement and success orientation of our society. It seems a particular disgrace that the uniqueness of kids is either overridden or suppressed by the frantic parents who insist upon normalizing their kids. Consider the bizarre case of New York City families, for example, who subjected their four-year-olds to IQ tests. They believe, evidently, that these tests will predispose their tiny children to Harvard or Yale by qualifying them now for New York City's elite private schools, one of which, apparently, is operated by Trinity parish. Ms. Axthelm, director of the Acorn School at 330 East 26th Street, seems a voice of sanity amid this hysteria. She puts the case that the test, to which these tykes must attend sometimes for an hour, frequently rules out the most resourceful kids. "They ask you to copy a block design," she says. "Some children would rather do their own design and be more creative. Guess what they get? Zero."[14]

But high IQ is not the only trophy of dubious worth for kids. Take that other indicator of highest achievement in U.S. society, celebrity status. There is actually an organization in our land called the American Academy of Achievement. Its members include Ralph Lauren, John Sununu, Ernest and Julio Gallo, and Michael Milken. (Okay, okay, maybe I went out of my way; there *are* others whom I associate with admirable achievement in this group.) But what they do is to convene by private jet and limo at a major U.S. city, as they did in San Francisco in June 1989, and, in the words of the *San Francisco Chronicle*, "like a collection of bees busily cross-pollinating . . . [they] chat over cocktails during numerous receptions, speak inspiring rhetoric to the star-struck [hand-picked high-school] students [gathered from around the country] and network like mad."[15] Sure I would love to have gone to such a thing when I was a high-school senior. If I had, I might have ended up making lots of money and gained some of this world's power. But that's the trouble. I know how moralistic this sounds, but we are called to something higher and better than all that. What we hold out to our kids as the epitome of success and achievement is very difficult to square with the story of the carpenter's son and what is written in the Bible, for instance, concerning how he wanted us to live. I am a hypocrite on this issue like all of us, but I do think the church's pastoral responsibilities to children includes encouraging them in their uniqueness, in the development of their God-given talents, and exposing the ways that clearly define the narcissistic, the fatuous, the shallow, the pagan. That previous attempts to do this were marked by self-righteousness, narrowness, bigotry, and no little amount of mental illness does not establish that the job still shouldn't be attempted again—perhaps this time with that quintessentially Anglican thing, good taste.

4. Ours would be a society in which what we call parenting is sincerely honored. The churches might be a good place to promote such an endeavor. Parents do matter an awful lot to kids. You knew that, and so did I. But we forget it in the everydayness of our lives. Jill Krementz's book *How It Feels When a Parent Dies* contains photographs of kids who lost a parent and her interviews of them. The kids range in age from nine to sixteen. A nine-year-old, for instance, says, "I still have dreams about my father—happy dreams. They make me feel good. And sometimes I see the light outside my window—it's on our garage—shining into my window, and I think it's Dad—his spirit. It's a secret. My mother doesn't know and my sisters don't know either. Nobody knows about it because the light only shines into my window. It makes me happy." There is an interview with a sixteen-year-old boy. His mother has died and he has talked about how he tries to be a brave (we would say, perhaps, macho) person. Then at the interview he talks about his father and how one day, after his mother died, the father had chest pains. He says, "I had a talk with him. I started crying and said, 'Dad, you've got to stop smoking. You have to pay attention to yourself because we love you and we don't want you to die. There's no one else after you.'"[16] Maybe you can see from these interviews how much kids need their parents—whether they know it or not and whether we

are aware of it or not. The enormously difficult business of making this point—that kids need their parents, both of them—is that divorced parents are frequently loaded with guilt, and anyway it is too late to rectify things. The important truth remains, however, as discovered by Judith Wallerstein over a twenty-year span, that divorce is devastating for kids and its effects persist well into adulthood. (A Census Bureau report, appearing in the March 2, 1991, *New York Times*, detailed the fact that "after their parents separate or divorce, children are almost twice as likely to be living in poverty than they were before the breakup . . .")

Nobody said marriage, or parenting, was easy. The pain of parenting is nicely brought out in this poem by Wyatt Prunty. It's called "Learning the Bicycle":

> The older children pedal past
> Stable as little gyros, spinning hard
> To supper, bath, and bed, until at last
> We also quit, silent and tired
> Beside the darkening yard where trees
> Now shadow up instead of down.
> Their predictable lengths can only tease
> Her as, head lowered, she walks her bike alone
> Somewhere between her wanting to ride
> And her certainty she will always fall.
> Tomorrow, though I will run behind,
> Arms out to catch her, she'll tilt then balance wide
> Of my reach, till distance makes her small,
> Smaller, beyond the place I stop and know
> That to teach her I had to follow
> And when she learned I had to let her go.[17]

Where more important to explore and celebrate these things, and support people in them, when there is precious little support for them in society, than in the churches? But it is just here that we could do more—more than teach kids the church school stories, though these should be taught, and more than try to boost their self-esteem and their relationship skills, though these should be attempted.

My friend Lew Smedes has been teaching ethics for a long time at Fuller Seminary in Pasadena. He's written a nifty book called

Mere Morality, and in it he proposes a Christian-ethics based bill of children's rights. These he specifies as the right to life, the right to care, the right to safety from abuse, the right to fairness, and the right to unconditional acceptance.[18] I suspect most church people would be willing to consider these in their own family life; these are as good a starting place as any, and they should be diligently explored with adults in the congregation. But church people should also work for their realization for all people—work in the public sector, where greed-based policy decisions make them all but impossible for the poor and the oppressed, the people and kids not always found in our comfortable churches.

I don't claim to be comprehensive in talking about our pastoral responsibilities concerning children. I am trying to quicken the sympathy we feel for children and our determination to make their lives richer, more fulfilling, in accordance with a Christian view of things. It is not only twelve-year-old Irene that I can't get out of my mind all these years later. It's all the others too. And it is the kids who come to the altar to receive the bread and wine some Sundays. It's the thirteen-year-old boy who passed me on his bicycle one day and said, with enormous pride of achievement, "I got my braces off!" I felt what an incalculable gift when a child shares something like that with you.

I'd like to end by telling you about one more kid. Shirley was fourteen years old when I met her. Her teacher had called me on the first day of school after Christmas vacation. Shirley had come into her office terribly upset, saying that her ten-year-old brother had been locked in a closet by their father since Christmas Eve. When I visited the school I heard more—how Shirley and her stepmother had brought food to the closet, how for years both kids had been severely beaten by their dad, and even more. The story was nearly unbelievable. As a protective-services employee I obtained an emergency pick-up order for both kids and placed them in emergency foster care. When the hearing came on to extend or revoke my custody of the kids I said to Shirley, "You must make a decision. You can testify against your father, telling the judge what you know of life inside your home. This might increase the chance that I can keep you in foster care; but I cannot guarantee how it will end up really. Maybe we would still fail, and then you would have to go back home. But you do not have to testify, and if you didn't, nobody would blame you." Shirley decided to testify against her dad. She looked tiny in the witness stand. Her father glowered at her. His attorney cross-examined the girl. The first day ended. I presented the same choice to her the next day. Again she testified. The hearing was interrupted, then continued a third day, and again she elected to testify to the truth as she knew it, placing her life (it is fair to say) on the line again and again. None of us knew whether the judge would order her returned to her father or whether she would go to the bleak circumstance of a foster home. The courage she showed throughout those days was something I had never seen before. I've never seen it since. The judge finally decided to keep her in the state's custody. We had "won"—if you call temporary foster care "winning." Both kids were safe for the time being. I asked Shirley why she testified against her dad. Without the slightest pretense she answered, "So my brother would have a chance to be a child."

Alyosha said, in *The Brothers Karamazov*,

> My dear children . . . you must know that there is nothing higher and stronger and more wholesome and good for life in the future than some good memory, especially a memory of childhood, or home. People talk to you a great deal about your education, but some good, sacred memory, preserved from childhood, is perhaps the best education. If one carries many such memories into life, one is safe to the end of one's days, and if one has only one good memory left in one's heart, even that may be the means to saving us.[19]

This fourteen-year-old would be around twenty-eight or twenty-nine today, if she is alive. Though I have no idea whatever happened to her, she inspires me as much today as she did then. She taught me by her example what's worth living and risking for. I'll never forget her, and because of her I'll never stop being an advocate for children. I hope you won't either.

DISCUSSION QUESTIONS

1. Is there a connection between the plight of children and special-interest lobbying in political centers for adult-serving outlays?
2. Name some instances of courage in children you know.

3. How do race, class, and gender affect the prospects of children in our society?
4. Is there a particular Christian duty concerning children?
5. Should a childless person have a concern about the children of others?
6. What should be the priorities and goals of public education of children?
7. What would a national children's policy look like?
8. In retrospect, would you do anything differently in respect to your own children, or would you have your parents do anything differently regarding you?

PEACEMAKING MINISTRY
IN BELLIGERENT TIMES

Christian leadership in peacemaking is never more urgently needed than in a time of war. Nor is it more difficult to accomplish than then. People don't know how to be for peace in wartime, especially when their most prominent political leaders are pounding the tom-toms of national belligerence. While writing a chapter on Anglican attitudes and behaviors concerning war for *The Anglican Moral Choice,* I discovered what we all know intuitively: Anglicans and Episcopalians are as good as any other mainline church in applying the rhetoric of peace to a world at peace . . . and in supporting war in a time of war!

Being faithful to the peace imperatives in wartime is tough, but that is when the issue is joined and the reflection of Christ's presence is needed most. Even though our presumed enemies may refuse to comply with our nation's demands, that does not mean that necessarily our first and only alternative is war. Because God calls us to reconciled community, war stands as a signal failure to Christians—morally, politically, and spiritually. Anyone trying to proclaim God's peaceful word will have difficulty engendering friendly thoughts about the presently designated enemy in particular. But since God loves even our enemies, talk of peace and reconciliation tends to remind us of what we have been unable to achieve, that from which we have departed; to a reflective mind this kind of talk hurts.

One of our country's most credible analysts of military affairs these days is Thomas Powers, who once wrote, "No one wants war, perhaps, but war is infinitely patient, and does not care what we want."[1] In this is the suggestion that wars have almost a mind of their own, their own initiative, their own autonomy. But of course war is a human invention, something we get too easily, I believe, because we haven't wanted peace enough, and the things that make for peace—like consideration for other people, a willingness to bear with them, an inclination to understand rather than demonize them. If you think about it, these things are among the suggestions for getting along with people that are scattered throughout the New Testament.

WAR'S VICTIMS

One of our difficulties with respect to war is that it is remote geographically. We have been spared its wrath in our country (since Appomattox at any rate) because we have been extremely lucky. But the resourcefulness of terrorists, and the fact that any country can attack us with chemical or biological agents, may change things. Years ago I worked briefly on a biological-warfare project for a major defense contractor. I learned that you don't even know you are under attack until you notice people starting to die. In theory one test tube of botulinus toxin, properly dispersed, can kill the human population of the planet. What we need, if only for self-interested reasons, is an urgency about peacemaking. This might be gained by considering war from the standpoint of its victims, or from the foot of the cross, if you like. (Indeed, apart from military promotions, war profits, and reelected politicians, I cannot think of many people who are *not* victims of war. Jeannette Rankin—no relation, unfortunately—is reported to have said, "You can no more win a war than you can win an earthquake.")

The first victims of war are the fighting personnel themselves. The February 3, 1991, *New York Times*, for instance, had an article entitled "War is Vivid in Gun Sights of the Sniper." In this a U.S. sergeant in Saudi Arabia—part of a crack marine sniper team—says, "When a sniper pulls the trigger, he can see the expression on a man's face when the bullet hits." He continues, "I try not to think about the other man's personal life. I concentrate on him being the enemy. If I were to give him sympathy I don't think I'd be very effective." Another sergeant says, "It is the art of killing. We have to be perfect." Still another sergeant speaks: "You put me anywhere and I can put it in the head from 800 yards."[2] Now I don't think we need to imagine Jesus saying things to recognize that there is something wrong here, in the operations these men perform, consciously or not, upon their own souls. Now I don't BLAME these men; it's just that the whole thing seems so terrible and sad. I find in their honesty an indication of the lethal spirituality authorized and nurtured by war and the preparations for war. Absent here is something central to the life-affirming, other-affirming, loving spirit of Christ. Whether damaged in body or soul, or both, military people are placed in gravest danger by war.

Civilians are among war's victims. I met a kind woman in Jerusalem a few years ago. She comes from an occupied West Bank town and is the widow of an Anglican clergyman. She said that Israeli doctors advised her and all other Palestinians to gather in a sealed inner room of their houses if a gas attack occurred. The Arab doctors, however, advised her to go outside and breathe deeply. The difference is between dying quickly or slowly. One recalls the famous words placed by Thucydides on the lips of the conquering Athenians: "The strong do what they can and the weak suffer what they must." There hardly exists in all literature a sentiment more precisely opposite to what Christ hoped for than that. But war does this.

Women are victims of war. This is a portion of a letter printed in the January 20, 1991, *New York Times*, written by Kate Millet, Robin Morgan, Gloria Steinem, and Ti-Grace Atkinson regarding the Gulf War: "This is not a war to defend democracy: Women in Kuwait cannot vote, no one in Saudi Arabia can vote, and women cannot even drive cars; a lesbian or homosexual is subject to barbarous methods of execution. This is not a war for any moral purpose, only for oil and power. . . . For twenty years we have said war is a feminist issue; it still is. Our priorities remain at home: poverty, racism, AIDS, the dangers to our economy, and ecology."[3] There is little disagreement that women in a destroyed country are among its greatest victims. The mothers, wives, sisters, and daughters of war's wounded and dead are themselves war's victims, wherever they live.

Parents are victims. I doubt there is a clergy person of my generation who has not sat with stunned and devastated parents as they tried to piece their lives together after a visit to their home by a military person in dress uniform. Sooner or later they must deal with the question: For what? For what did our son or daughter suffer and die?

Children. Even the kids who grow up safe, healthy, and protected at home can be victimized terribly by a far-off war. Consider this note left at the Vietnam Memorial in Washington: "Even though I never really knew you, you still meant the world to me. Thank you, Daddy, for giving me three years of your life. Remembering you through photos, I can only say I love you, Daddy. Happy Father's Day. Part of me died with you. Love, Your son Joe."[4]

I was in Jerusalem just before the Iraqi invasion of Kuwait. I visited the children's memorial at Yad Vashem. It is dark inside, with mirrors placed so as to reflect, seemingly a million and a half times, the flames of tiny candles—one for each of the 1.5 million Jewish children killed in the 1930s and 1940s. A woman's voice reads in English the names of the children who are known, the age at the time of death, and the country of each child. I wanted to bring all the world's leaders inside this memorial and ask them to commit to world peace.

WAR, PEACE, AND THE ETHICS OF CHARACTER

In the tradition of Christian moral theology are found character-ethics terms like honor, integrity, courage, faithfulness, caritas, and the like. I want to examine some of these as they apply to individuals and nations in the war context.

The word *honor,* for instance, is frequently used in militaristic contexts, where it describes certain virtues consonant with the military task. (I hasten to say, incidentally, that I have much respect and affection for many military people I know; my problem is not with them, but with the larger "principality and power" of *militarism,* which I understand to be a societal—not necessarily a military—tendency to solve problems by force rather than, say, diplomacy.) The term *honor,* anyway, can as easily be reframed within a Christian context. There it might mean what E. L. Doctorow meant in the open letter he wrote to our president in January 1991. He said, "A modern nation's honor is not the honor of a warrior; it is the honor of a father providing for his children, it is the honor of a mother providing for HER children."[5]

Or take the notion of integrity. How are we to conceive of integrity in governmental leadership in wartime when reports such as this come into view: "White House communications director Pat Buchanan, who first called the contras 'the moral equivalent of the Founding Fathers,' missed military service with a bad knee. Georgia Congressman Newt Gingrich, columnist George Will, Assistant Secretary of Defense Richard Pearle, Secretary of the Navy John Lehman—all unabashed advocates of protecting our interests abroad with the blood of American boys—ducked service in Vietnam with college deferments . . ."[6] I do not wish to be unduly harsh concerning all political leaders. One hopes they feel the burden of protecting the nation in appropriate ways when it is truly threatened. My interest just now is in the possibility that beneath the surface of war rhetoric may lie some issues of integrity that should be analyzed for their possible implications for the country as a whole, and for those in presently defined enemy countries as well. Integrity also requires that there be some substantial integration of Christian pronouncements, actions, and attitudes with the central elements of the Christian heritage concerning war and peace. (Of this I will say more below in my discussion of the Gulf war.)

Courage. The relevant meanings of this moral, theological term are usefully brought out in a Johns Hopkins speech a few years ago by David Cornwell—a spy-story writer best known under his pen name, John LeCarre. He said, "It's not, after all, the dissenters who have brought havoc to our non-conciliatory world, but the LOYAL men [sic] marching blindly to the music of their institutionalized faiths: THEIR record is not good, whether they are marching to the posthumous tunes of the British Empire, for Islam, for Germany (whichever one), for God (whomever he is working for at the moment), or for democracy of whatever brand." Cornwell concludes, "The only thing we can say in safety, perhaps, is that the greatest threat to mankind comes from the renunciation of individual scruple in favor of institutional denominators; from the adoption of slogan, and the mute acceptance of prepackaged animosities, in preference to the hard-fought decisions of individual conscience. Real heroism lies, as it always will, not in conformity or even patriotism but in acts of solitary moral courage. Which, come to think of it, is what we used to admire in our Christian savior."[7] I believe the social approbation attached to military courage explains why idealistic and altruistic people make such extraordinary sacrifices in violent endeavors. The Christian community, however, beginning with its leaders, needs to approve acts of solitary witness and idiosyncrasy in the service of nonviolence and peacemaking as well.

BAD FAITH OR LUCIDITY

The theological and ethical—and I would say, spiritual—phenomenon that I find most worrisome in wartime is what Sartre called "bad faith." Times of war especially spawn this. The term refers to the way the "Night and Fog" of managed information, press censorship, contradictory reports, and plain old self-serving denial causes people to censor themselves. They remain passive and thus complicit in the ongoing destruction of violence, even though, deep down, they know that what is occurring is wrong. From a Christian perspective, the corrosion of the self's integrity engendered by this process is spiritual injury. Simone Weil reported this fearsome truth, that we do have the capacity to harm our own souls, even mortally. When people lie to themselves in wartime, this process is already underway.

On the other hand, clarity, honesty, "lucid knowledge" characterize the healthy soul. Philip Hallie, an ethics teacher, traces the gemlike moral clarity of the people of Le Chambon, a tiny protestant mountain village in southern France. Here an entire community worked together, at considerable risk and with enormous dedication, to save numbers of Jews from the Nazis. Despite incentives to go along with the common practice of reporting Jews to the authorities, these people instead cleaved to a few simple principles. They also were strongly under the influence of their clergy leaders. They determined never to harm anyone in any way if they could possibly avoid doing so. They appropriated the commandment against killing anyone for any reason. They committed themselves to the love commandment. Hallie describes the lucid and principled honesty of these people: "There was no fog for them because they cared enough to see and to act and to be firm. . . . That mixture of lucid knowledge, awareness of the pain of others, and stubborn decision dissipated for the Chambonnais the Night and Fog that inhabited the minds of so many people in Europe, and the world at large, in 1942."[8] Of the pastor who presided over this Christian community Hallie writes, "With his sophisticated mind, he put his sophisticated mind aside and chose to be a Kindler, who would not kill and would not betray."[9]

There is a peculiarly subtle trick Christian leaders—especially clergy—can play on themselves, which in the rising tide of war fever can constitute, I think, "bad faith." This is the tendency to overindulge acts of small charity to the point that no freedom is left to be concerned with the larger issue. The idea was put memorably by Bonhoeffer, I think it was, who said that in certain moments the issue is not to patch up the victims crushed by the wheel, but to stop the wheel in the first place. I have seldom been more moved than when reading the poems and prayers of Peguy. In *The Mystery of the Charity of Joan of Arc* he takes up the extent to which our acts of individual charity—one might say, small *"p"* pastoring—no matter how admirable, meet the case in the large, twisted context of violence. Here is part of a dialogue between Peguy's Joan and Madame Gervaise:

> *Gervaise:* My child, charity is never useless.
> *Joan:* And don't do anything about it except for useless
> charity, as long as we don't want to kill war we just go
> along with it. We let the soldiers do what they want, so we,
> you, can't escape this, we are torturers and we are damners
> of souls as well.
> Just to go along with it is the same as sticking in the
> knife yourself.
> He who lets it be done is the same as he who does it. It's
> the same thing. . . . It's even worse than being the one who
> sticks in the knife. For the one who does it, he who does do
> a crime, at least he has the courage to do it. But when you
> let something be done, that's just the same thing; and
> that's just . . . feeble, feeble, feeble . . . that cowardice.[10]

It is quite easy, and in a superficial way virtuous, for Christian leaders to fill their plates with small *"p"* pastoring, administration, charity, and the like, until there is no time for what may matter more in terms of the larger and tougher concerns of peacemaking. Insofar as this is tied to denial and suppression of the harder truths, it would be an instance of bad faith.

Christian peacemaking leadership in the time of emerging war fever is difficult because then is when nationalism is most strident. Its spirituality fills the air we breathe and it intoxicates. Religiously speaking, this is the power of idolatry. In 1968, a time of frightening upheaval over the Vietnam War, Arnold Toynbee wrote, "The cult [of national sovereignty] has become mankind's major religion. . . . Today, the nation state is a god, [for sovereignty], when one analyzes its implications, means divinity, nothing less."[11] Do we need more proof of our enthrallment to this God of death? Are the deaths of 70 million people killed in war in this first half-century enough to convince us?

Thus war and war fever are profoundly a religious matter. The gods of nation and war summon the worshipful allegiance of even the best among us. The opposing religion is centered around the Prince of Peace, the servant, the preacher of neighbor and even enemy love. The religious issue of who or what is ultimately sovereign is most clearly joined while the drumbeats of war begin to erode common sense, common decency, and reasonable restraint. Our most recent experience of this is the war against Iraq. What was that about? What lessons emerge from that for Christian peacemakers today?

THE GULF WAR: CAUSES AND RATIONALES

Only a few years have passed since the end of the largest international crisis of the post–Cold War period. A quarter of a million people are reported to have died—one way or another—in the time following the largest assault force since the invasion of Normandy was launched, buttressed by the most intense aerial bombardment in history. Repeatedly we were told the war against Iraq was just; but was it? Since the pullout of the nearly half a million U.S. military personnel from the Gulf we are now offered a chance to gain some perspective upon what George Bush named "the defining moment for a new world order." What in fact seem to have been the causes of our military involvement in that region?

The immediate, stated reason offered by President Bush for his decision to involve U.S. forces in the region was the Iraqi invasion of Kuwait, and the Iraqi leader's presumed intention to go on to invade Saudi Arabia. This reason was advanced as late as November 8, 1991, when in response to skepticism over whether such involvement was worth the risk to U.S. lives President Bush remarked that if the Democrats could have had their way the U.S. would be sitting "fat, dumb and happy with Saddam Hussein maybe in Saudi Arabia."[12] But whether Saddam Hussein would indeed have gone into Saudi Arabia is "questionable," according to Theodore Draper. Even if Iraq had once posed a threat to Saudi Arabia, the decision to send U.S. military might was made after that threat had clearly subsided.[13]

President Bush's August 8, 1990, statement as to his intentions and their rationale was confusing in that he justified the deployment that day of the first 82nd Airborne troops in Saudi Arabia as a "wholly defensive" event; yet Mr. Bush also insisted upon "the immediate, unconditional and complete withdrawal of all Iraqi forces from Kuwait."[14] How the *defensive* positioning of U.S. troops in Saudi Arabia connected logically with Iraq's voluntary withdrawal from Kuwait was a mystery.

By August 21, a new element appeared in the picture. That day the president said, "I don't rule in or rule out the use of force." Within a few weeks President Bush's position seemed to have been modified further: On September 11 the president's speech to a joint session of Congress contained no mention of defending Saudi Arabia; he now spoke only of dislodging Iraq from Kuwait.[15] That the main purpose of the U.S. military deployment was to liberate Kuwait was announced again by the president on October 16, 1990, when he said, "The fight isn't about oil; the fight is about naked aggression that will not stand."[16]

Possibly in anticipation of the question as to whether liberating Kuwait was worth risking U.S. lives, George Bush had earlier provided a somewhat expansive reason for fighting against Iraq. On August 15, 1990, he said that "Our jobs, our way of life, our own freedom, and the freedom of friendly countries around the world will suffer if control of the world's great oil reserves fell in the hands of that one man, Saddam Hussein."[17]

But maybe out of continued concern over the skepticism expressed in the instant antiwar slogan, "no blood for oil," President Bush in February 1991 announced that the Iraqi invasion of Kuwait "pose[d] an unusual and extraordinary threat to the national security and foreign policy of the United States."[18] This, however, did not make a lot of sense to a number of critics.

Clarity concerning the need to risk U.S. lives in a war—or, to those sensitized to such things, clarity regarding the need to risk *anyone's* life in war—was apparently perceived as needed by James

Baker. Therefore on November 13, 1990, the president's secretary of state said it was time to explain the necessity of going to war by bringing it "down to the level of the average American citizen." The reason for going to war, in one word, he said, was "jobs."[19] But the secretary's meaning eluded some people still. The Senate Minority Leader, Robert Dole, tried his hand at it. He said there was a simple way to grasp the need for war, and he spelled out that need— "O-I-L."[20] The discrepancies in stated and disavowed, then restated, reasons for going to war in the Gulf proved unsettling to some of the people who paid much attention at all to what was being said.

■　■　■

The advantage of hindsight may complicate, as well as clarify, the reasons for the war. Sometimes, however, one is left only with speculations, and these notoriously say more about the speculator than the situation itself. A leading theory intending to explain U.S. military involvement in the Gulf holds that it served to provide renewed financial enrichment to what President Eisenhower called the military-industrial complex—a consortium of economic and po-litical interests that momentarily faced an uncertain future due to the end of the Cold War. This theory holds that President Bush was committed to keeping domestic military expenditures at the highest possible levels, while promoting arms sales overseas as vigorously as possible. This effort is thought to have been animated further by political pressures from constituencies economically dependent upon arms manufacturing. Steven Elliot-Gower of the University of Georgia's Center for East-West Trade Policy is one such theorist. He has stated that the Bush administration ordered U.S. embassies to expand their help to the U.S. arms industry and sought federal guarantees for nearly $1 billion in loans for our allies to purchase weapons.[21] The resupply of weapons to various Gulf states was also an obvious boon to U.S. arms manufacturers.

Still another hypothesis offered for why the U.S. went to war against Iraq is psychologically based. It holds that George Bush wanted to be the president remembered for restoring U.S. national pride after the presumably shameful debacle of Vietnam. (The psy-chology of national disgrace is sometimes referred to as the "Vietnam syndrome.") This theory holds that beginning with President Reagan's invasion of Grenada in 1983, then President Bush's invasion of Panama in 1990, a process was underway to find a next suitable opponent to reestablish, once and for all, U.S. military supremacy in the world. The assumption was that military preeminence is good for the American psyche. Thus one journal editorialized: "To end the Vietnam syndrome, Bush desperately wanted a more substantial war, one that could be sold on the basis of high principle and that could demonstrate this country's overwhelming military power at a low cost in American lives—in short, a war that could justify the continued efforts to control the destinies of lesser nations, as well as the ongoing militarization of American society that such efforts require. It was Hussein's mistake [in invading Kuwait] that granted Bush this opportunity on a silver platter."[22] The "real" reason for the war with Iraq, according to this view, had to do with a presumed national psychological need, and with an identifiable psychological need on the part of the president and his advisors.

■　■　■

One can rule out as a reason for our going to war the Iraqi capacity for developing a nuclear weapon, since this only clearly emerged after the war's conclusion. (The details of Iraq's progress in the nuclear endeavor, and lack thereof, came to light only after the seventh U.N. Special Commission's visit to Baghdad on September 22, 1991. This team discovered documents at the "Petrochemical Three" (PC-3) office there, and also verified the patent attempts by Iraqi leaders to deceive the U.N. concerning the nuclear project's true status.)[23]

A curious event occurred in October 1990. An anonymous Kuwaiti girl testified tearfully and poignantly to the House Human Rights Caucus in Washington that she had personally seen Iraqi soldiers remove fifteen infants from incubators in a Kuwait City hospital and leave them to die on the hospital's cold floor. After this testimony, from a teenager whose anonymity was guaranteed because of an alleged need to insulate her family against reprisals, several senators announced their support for our going to war; they explicitly cited her statement as central to their decisions. But on January 6, 1991, *Harper's* magazine publisher John MacArthur disclosed that the girl was in fact the daughter of the Kuwaiti ambassador to the United States. Moreover, she had been brought to the committee hearings by a vice president of the nation's largest advertising firm, Hill and Knowlton. This firm's clients were an organization known as Citizens for a Free Kuwait, and its major funding source was apparently the emir of Kuwait.

The Kuwaiti girl's testimony was reconsidered in light of some other questions. Among these were: Should we really believe that the daughter of the Kuwaiti ambassador to the U.S. was in a Kuwait City hospital in August and September of 1990, after the Iraqi invasion? Even if so, how did she escape, and why hasn't that story been told? Perhaps most damning, why would her identity as the Kuwaiti ambassador's daughter have been kept secret—really—from the U.S. Congress? The child is shielded from reporters even to this day. Meanwhile an advertising-industry publication has reported an $11 million payment to Hill and Knowlton, the incident has been scrutinized by the CBS show "Sixty Minutes," and there is some public discussion in the advertising industry about the ethical implications of the difference between advertising and propagandizing.[24]

Altogether, it seems safe to say that the real reason or reasons that the U.S. went to war against Iraq are still somewhat unclear. President Bush and his colleagues gave different explanations. Sometimes, indeed, these explanations seemed disingenuous, as for instance when appeal was made to international laws—because U.S. government respect for international laws during the past decade or longer has not otherwise been noticeably ardent. Confusion arose in the face of public uncertainty over which group or groups in our country would benefit significantly from a war.

One thing was always true: Saddam Hussein was an overwhelmingly unlikable figure. His invasion of Kuwait was a brutal act of aggression, though it should be evaluated by reference to the larger historical context of boundary disputes and a well-recognized Arab disdain for Kuwaiti smugness and arrogance. Saddam Hussein's documented cruelty and his need for oil constituted a valid concern for world leaders. But still the question remains, why was the U.S. leader demonstrably more exercised against the Iraqi leader than were most other world leaders? Further, if we are supposed to accept that the liberation of Kuwait and the establishment of a just peace were the true motives for U.S. involvement in the Gulf War, there is still the nagging fact that our country has for a very long time "tolerated injustice as long as the oil flowed."[25] So another question is forced to consciousness: Why the outrage *at this time?*

Questions like these linger, at least for those who think about them. They are troublesome not only in themselves, but in the fact that they did not protect the great majority of U.S. citizens from war fever, once the president made it clear that war is what he wanted. There is some thought that the administration's close support of Iraq during the terrible Iran-Iraq war led the U.S. president to expect complete loyalty from Saddam Hussein. When the Iraqi leader went into Kuwait, according to this view, President Bush felt personally betrayed and infuriated. Whatever were the exact reasons for the decision to go to war, the approximately 50 percent of U.S. citizens who had been opposed became relatively silent once it was underway. David S. Cunningham, writing in a Christian journal of opinion, stated: "The public obsession with war seemed to overpower the traditional Christian resources for talking about peace. Pastoral calls for restraint were largely ignored; flocks were too transfixed by military briefers and bandwagoning movie stars. An overwhelming majority of U.S. Christians seemed more attuned to arguments based on political expediency than to arguments based on the life and work of Jesus Christ."[26]

When the decision was actually made to take the U.S. into war, an effective—some would say cynical—process was undertaken to align the United Nations firmly in its support. In all likelihood Egypt's debt to the U.S. was reduced by about $7 billion and its debt to the Gulf states reduced by $6.7 billion for its U.N. vote in favor of war against Iraq. For its vote Syria received $200 million from the European Community, $500 million in Japanese loans, and over $2 billion from Saudi Arabia and other Arab nations. Turkey's $500 million in annual U.S. military aid was fortified for its support, and the Soviet Union was given $1 billion by the Saudis and it also obtained U.S. credit guarantees. China's willingness not to veto the U.N. plan was rewarded by a White House reception for its foreign minister—the first such gesture in the year and a half following the massacre in Tiananmen Square. Not all the world community, however, swung into line: because of its stubborn unwillingness to go along with the plan, Yemen's $70 million in U.S. foreign aid was cancelled.[27]

RESULTS

Clearly the chief result of the Gulf War was the removal of Iraqi soldiers from Kuwait, which was a major objective of the U.S. government. With or without enormous weapons superiority, as a matter of military strategy and tactics this must be regarded as an impressive achievement. Moreover, the growing military power of Iraq in the region has been significantly set back because of the war, at least for the time being. Another major result is a new opportunity for Iran to exercise its influence in the region—an influence that may be felt primarily to the north in the Islamic republics of the old Soviet Union.

A vexing question has to do, however, with the degree to which the Kuwaiti government has become more civilized now that the war is over. In the editorial contained in the October 1990 *Bulletin of the Atomic Scientists*, for instance, the editor noted that "there is no democracy to restore in Kuwait. Before Iraq's August 2 invasion it was a feudal, oil-rich oligarchy operated for the benefit of the ostentatious al-Sabah family. A U.S. State Department fact sheet labels Kuwait a "constitutional monarchy," with an elected fifty-member National Assembly. The sheet notes, however, that the only eligible voters are "adult males who resided in Kuwait before 1920 and their male descendants." In 1988 they totalled 56,848 voters, 8.3 percent of the citizenry."[28]

Outside the Gulf and Middle East, however, at least in the shorter run, the war's importance is not likely to be regarded as great. Instead the breaking apart of the Soviet Union, and the apparent end of the Cold War, seem to be more fraught with significance for the world than are the fortunes of either Iraq or Kuwait. Even within the region itself a decades-long set of problems has not been resolved; these have to do with border disputes between Iraq and Kuwait, ownership and/or control of the two offshore islands claimed by both countries, and ownership of various parts of the Rumaila oil fields. The war also contributed to the continued undermining of Arab and pan-Arab identity.

Examining Kuwait somewhat more closely, one discovers that upon its liberation from Iraqi army occupation, its government expelled hundreds of thousands of non-Kuwaiti workers as "enemy subjects." This was done without legal trials. Those kicked out included Palestinians, Yemenis, Jordanians, and Sudanese—all now newly created refugees presently dispersed throughout the entire Middle East and constituting "a vast human calamity."[29]

An obvious consequence of the war is the environmental devastation of Kuwait, caused by Iraqi soldiers setting fire to its oil wells. The damage to the environment is unprecedented. A special report by Richard Golob, appearing in the January-February *Harvard Magazine*, stated that "Altogether Kuwait lost through spillage and fire more than five thousand times as much oil as the *Exxon Valdez* tanker spilled into Prince William Sound."[30] According to Golob, the toxic pollutants from the fires will likely be a health problem of considerable proportions for the people there, as will be the undetonated military ordnance remaining in the area—much of it in unknown locations.

A factor in the origin of the war was Arab resentment and envy of the Kuwaiti leadership. Did the war's destruction change official Kuwaiti attitudes and behaviors? Theodore Draper analyzes the lessons learned and not learned by the Kuwaiti government: "Kuwait was and remains an anomaly. Its rulers show no sincere signs of having learned anything or forgotten anything, despite their near disaster. . . . To defend them against aggression is not the same as to deal with the problems which brought about the aggression."[31]

PRECISION BOMBING AND HIGH-TECH WEAPONRY

Much has been made of the precision bombing, or lack of it, in the Gulf War. U.S. military leaders have been outspoken in their insistence that bombing "point" rather than "area" targets made possible by precision bombing was a way of making the conduct of the war more just. What are the results, really? A report, *Needless Deaths in the Gulf War*, by Middle East Watch, chronicles the military-induced destruction of the country of Iraq. In the opinion of one commentator, the document "is sickening to read. The destruction of Iraq's electrical system, communications facilities, factories, railroads, waterways, bridges, and highways—in fact the entire infrastructure—showed that bombing could not be limited to military targets only."[32]

In truth approximately 85,000 tons of "conventional" bombs fell on Iraq and Kuwait during the war, an equivalent in destructive power to five Hiroshimas. Weapons expert Michael T. Klare states that "Comparable quantities of rockets, missiles and artillery shells were also fired during the Persian Gulf war, making it the most firepower-intensive conflict since World War II."[33]

The nature of the high-tech weapons is important to understand. They were originally developed for use against the Soviet Union or its Eastern European allies, but were first used in the Gulf War. The history of their development is relatively simple: Initially the prospect of spending the money necessary to give Europe-based NATO forces military superiority over Soviet-backed Warsaw Pact forces was not palatable to either European or U.S. voters. A different strategy was therefore developed to enable the sought-after parity to be achieved at a relatively smaller economic cost. This was accomplished by "nuclearizing" existing NATO weapons. But then rising public opposition to nuclear weapons, and especially to their use on European soil, finally led to the development of "conventional" weapons that delivered the punch of tactical nuclear weapons or were accurate enough to destroy the other side's weapons, or both. The weapons developed in response to these considerations were what were used in Iraq, especially against "high-value" targets like command and control centers, air fields, and armored-vehicle formations.

A few of the more celebrated of the high-tech weapons used in the Gulf include the Multiple-Launch Rocket System. This system had not been used in actual combat before the war in the Gulf. It is a transportable container capable of delivering twelve rockets on target twenty miles away in under a minute. It disperses about 7,700 bomblets over an area comprising six football fields. Although "bomblet" sounds almost cute and benign, it is anything but. Upon detonation each bomblet hurls at high speed small bits of steel shrapnel capable of shredding human bodies and severely damaging many kinds of vehicles. This shrapnel is known to U.S. soldiers as "steel rain." The cost per missile is about $100,000, or $1.2 million for a system of twelve.

Another weapon is the Army Tactical Missile System. This is a surface-to-surface missile that can travel about sixty-five miles and convey 950 bomblets. It is more expensive than the Multiple-Launch Rocket System, however. It costs $615,000 per missile. Other weapons include the Tomahawk sea-launched cruise missile, fired from both surface ships and submarines. It can travel 700 nautical miles while carrying a 1,000-pound warhead. Although touted as highly accurate against "point" targets, many of these missed their targets altogether in Kuwait and Iraq and struck civilian structures instead. They cost $1.4 million each.

The SLAM (Standoff Land-Attack Missile) is fired from an aircraft "standing off" a safe distance from its target. It delivers a 500-pound warhead over sixty nautical miles, guided by a "Walleye" video system enabling the pilot to bring the warhead in on a point target. This costs $1.1 million each. The Laser-Guided Bomb is familiar to anyone who watched television news reports during the war. It is a 2,000-pound bomb designed to home in on a laser beam aimed by an aircraft crew member at a "point" target. Despite the impression given by military personnel to the media, many of these bombs missed their targets and struck civilian structures, causing enormous damage and loss of life.

The Fuel-Air Explosive is a large bomb filled with highly volatile fuels and an explosive charge. The fuels are dispersed over a wide area, where they hang in the air like a cloud. The cloud is then ignited and forms a massive firestorm that consumes the air itself. A CIA report concludes, "The pressure effects of Fuel-Air Explosives approach those produced by low-yield nuclear weapons at short ranges."[34] Entirely apart from their use in the Gulf, these weapons are worrisome to some because other nations are known to replicate U.S. weaponry within a few years, and the thought that F.A.E.s would be used by other nations raises moral concerns not evidently raised by U.S. military leaders and applied to themselves. Some are worried now that with F.A.E.s and perhaps other high-tech weapons, the U.S. has opened a Pandora's box like the one it first opened with atomic weapons in 1945, and then with thermonuclear weapons after that. Bigger and better weapons sell, and then they must be sold again to presumed enemies for the sake of parity. This is the inner dynamic of arms-racing and weapons-profiteering. At the moment, unfortunately, according to Michael Klare, "few restraints govern the newer conventional weapons."[35]

Withal, an important result of the Gulf War is the introduction of a new class of horrific nonnuclear weapons. In all likelihood they will become standard shelf items in the armories of increasing numbers of countries. What we hoped we were gaining in the restraint of nuclear weapons we now seem to be losing in the design, manufacture, and sale of high-tech "conventional" weapons of monstrous destructive potential.

■   ■   ■

CIVIL LIFE IN IRAQ

The picture of destruction and despair in Iraq becomes clearer with the release of each successive report. In March 1991, for instance, a U.N. report described Iraq bomb damage as "near apocalyptic." It went on to predict the near reduction of "a rather highly urbanized and mechanized society to a preindustrial age."[36] One month later a Harvard contingent discovered in Iraq "a public health catastrophe due to the cumulative effects of the Allied bombing and resulting sanctions."[37] In July the United Nations estimated that "50–80 thousand infants are at risk of severe malnutrition because of the war."[38] By August 1991 an international team containing specialists and researchers in several fields, and coming from over a dozen countries, found an abysmal public-health problem in Iraq. The greatest suffering was being felt by "children, elderly, women, and the poor." Food is absent, children play in raw sewage. And the same children are, in the words of two world-famous child psychologists, "the most traumatized children of war ever described." Economically "real earnings are less [in Iraq] than 7 percent of what they were before the start of the Gulf crisis.[39] Dr. Tim Cote of the National Cancer Institute reported Iraq's child-mortality rate has more than tripled since the war's end. Nearly a million Iraqi children under five years of age are "significantly undernourished." Further, "two-thirds of school age children believe they will not live to adulthood."[40]

In testimony given to the House Select Committee on Hunger on November 13, 1991, Jim McDermott, both a physician and a U.S. Congressman, noted that U.S. policy in imposing sanctions was to precipitate the "downfall of Saddam Hussein." But given the enormous suffering of the Iraqi people, "we must ask ourselves, at what point does the starvation of 18 million people take precedence over our attempts to remove one person from power?" McDermott went on: "Starving the people of Iraq will not topple Saddam Hussein. He is eating, and his advisors and the Republican Guard are eating. Hussein will continue to hold out, and I do not doubt that he is willing to let the Iraqi people starve in the process. We are confronted with an ethical and moral dilemma: What is more important—feeding the Iraqi children or opposing Saddam? I believe a majority of the American people would overwhelmingly support providing humanitarian aid to the children of Iraq."[41] (One might also inquire whether the alleged deaths of the fifteen Kuwait City hospital children—even if they did occur—somehow are vindicated by what is now happening in Iraq.)

By January 15, James Fine was pleading in *The Christian Century* for an easing of U.S. and U.N. sanctions against Iraq. Fine pointed to U.N. Situation Report No. 18, issued in December 1991, and to other U.N. reports documenting the public-health disaster occurring there. As of December the water and sewage facilities that our bombers had destroyed had still not been repaired, there were "massive shortages of basic drugs" and other vital medical supplies, food prices were at fifteen to twenty times the prewar levels, and that about 15 million gallons of raw sewage were flowing each hour into the Tigris River from Baghdad alone. Since there is little likelihood of toppling Saddam Hussein anyway, and since allowing "limited oil sales to finance urgently needed humanitarian supplies" seems a compassionate and reasonable response, if not to say a refreshing alternative to wreaking havoc upon that nation, the merciful alternative was recommended.[42]

By February 23, 1992, the *New York Times* reported the results of the Pentagon's own study, which disclosed bomb damage to Iraq's civilian infrastructure far greater than intended. This was caused apparently by communications malfunctions that prevented air units from receiving precise and current targeting information. The Pentagon admitted "enormous damage to power plants, causing the shutdown of sewage-treatment and water-purification plants, and slowed medical services after the war." The study's conclusions included that only 10 percent of the bombs used in the Gulf were the supposedly precise "smart" bombs.[43]

The special vulnerability of the Kurds and minority Shi'ites in Iraq was made more severe by U.S. encouragement to rebel, followed by the withdrawal of the U.S. and U.N. forces that might have protected them against subsequent reprisal. Philosopher Russell Sizemore believes that "we have a responsibility for the safety of the people we have jeopardized. We could have grounded Hussein's helicopter gunships and fixed-wing aircraft and reduced his slaughter of civilians. We may not have the wisdom to remake Iraqi society, but we could have minimized a massacre."[44]

IMAGES OF THE U.S.

An ethics perspective entails an interest in the question, What can be inferred about the national character of the U.S. from the war against Iraq? What did we convey about who we are and what we intend as a people? The answers to these questions are of course dependent upon one's subjective assessment of the overall situation. One observer, Professor Lopez of Notre Dame University, believes that our government's unwillingness even now to discuss casualties, civilian or military, "leaves the sense that the American conscience cannot focus on American errors and responsibilities."[45] Even as independent agencies release reports of the war's devastation, there is a marked silence from official U.S. sources on this subject. U.S. silence is interpreted by some skeptical analysts as evidence of a "destroy-and-abandon" policy, which makes it of a piece with Panama, Nicaragua, and Lebanon.[46]

Even the glory that the military would like to heap on itself because of its rapid and thorough success is suspect: "It was not a glorious victory and could not have been a glorious victory against an enemy that was so outclassed and did not fight."[47] Indeed, "As for the United States, it proved little more than that it can smite an opponent like Iraq in short order."[48] And perhaps more troublesome, from an international point of view, when the opportunity arose to try to structure a newer, better Iraq, no effort was made to do so. This was a political failure of nerve, and it left Saddam Hussein in power. This, according to Draper, "signified that we could dominate the region militarily but could not lead it politically."

Within the U.S. itself, a worrisome message was conveyed to all concerning the military's value of U.S. children. Professor Jean Bethke Elshtain, quoting from Defense Department figures, wrote in a *Christian Century* article that 17,500 U.S. families were left without any custodial parent to care for the children due to the call-up of military parents, mostly women in this case. Elshtain remarks, "Just war politics suggests . . . that we consider the sobering possibility that a society that puts the needs of its children dead last is a society 'progressing' rapidly toward moral ruin."[49]

The unprecedented military control of the press during the Gulf War has occasioned comment on the role of information in a free democracy. The evidence indicates that certain favored reporters were given more information by local commanders than were other newspeople. The military seemed to be operating from a view that the press's role in undermining public support for the Vietnam War was not going to be allowed to happen again. In a low point for press censorship, "An Associated Press photographer, Scott Applewhite, was handcuffed, beaten, and had one of his cameras smashed by US and Saudi military policemen when he photographed the crash of an Iraqi Scud missile on a barracks near Dharan."[50]

Reflecting on the overall problem, novelist E. L. Doctorow wrote, "Never before, not in the First or Second World Wars, not in Korea or Vietnam, has the American press been subject to such debasement and humiliation. The historical record shows that under conditions of the widest media latitude in those wars, including the war in Vietnam, only a small number of minor reportorial transgressions occurred of a degree damaging to military operations." Doctorow explores the possible reasons for the tight control: "It was not for reasons of military security that reporters were denied access to Dover Air Force Base, Delaware, where the bodies of GIs were brought home for transshipment to their families." Rather the concern was upon the reactions of the U.S. public, whose support was needed to sustain the war effort: "Docility was what [Bush] wanted from us and that is what he made sure he got."[51]

Finally, on the subject of the U.S. itself, Theodore Draper writes, "One domestic aspect of the war may have the most far-reaching consequences of all, because it touches the constitutional fabric of the nation. Other presidents have reached out for more and more power but not until George Bush did any president openly proclaim that he and he alone could decide on taking the country into war."[52] This kind of precedent, says Draper, "will haunt this country far longer than the Gulf War will remain a vivid memory." He fears that if it remains unchallenged, "it represents a constitutional watershed that future generations will look back at with wonder that it could have slipped through so easily."[53]

The immediate effects of the Gulf War victory were entirely positive in the United States. Lengthier reflection, however, may give rise to deeper, ethical concerns about who we are and what we are perhaps becoming.

A JUST WAR?

The presumption of just war theory is that war is wrong and should always be avoided if at all possible; this is why fighting a war must meticulously be justified in the first place. A pacifistic view of war's implicit wrongness is thus presupposed: there is the clear recognition that the effects of war are so dreadful that they could well overwhelm the good that originally was sought; there is the stout insistence that killing people in war—as in peacetime—makes people killers. There is in church circles the awareness that Christ did not go around killing people, or counseling others to do so, and that therefore waging war implicitly contravenes fundamental religious convictions and principles. The just war, in other words, is not a loosely applied checklist of incidental things to do in the course of preparing for war.

A noted Christian scholar, for instance, characterizes the Jesus ethic as uniquely an insistence upon loving one's neighbors: This ethic "permits no distinctions between personal enemies and national enemies, everyday experiences, religious conflicts, or military options. . . . The conquering power of love is limited by no boundary. . . . The command of love knows no condition and no presupposition; it is valid for every place and every time."[54] The stringency of this is supposed to make the justification of war a very precise matter indeed.

A markedly different approach to war, however, which has been exhibited in world politics—and not only by Arabs—is the holy war or, in Christian trappings, the crusade. The chief characteristic of this approach is the assumption that God is on one's side, against the other side. Jean Bethke Elshtain believes President Bush both assimilated and propagated this motif: "For example, the president spoke of 'good vs. evil, right vs. wrong, human dignity and freedom vs. tyranny and oppression.' He equated our 'just cause' with a 'noble cause,' a bit of crowing that more sober just war thinkers steadfastly avoided. The U.S. and its coalition were 'on the side of God,' he declared, although just war doctrine insists that God's ways are forever hidden to us. . . ."[55]

Three of the most hotly debated criteria of the just war, as they were publicly discussed in the context of the Iraq war, are that the war must be fought as a last resort, that discrimination must be employed in differentiating military from civilian targets (and do no harm to the latter), and that proportionality be employed to make more likely that the harm done in war be less than the resulting gains.

To take these principles in order, was the war in fact a last resort? Had every means of diplomacy and peaceful resolution been exhausted before the shooting began? The war's critics, including some former military chiefs of staff (Admiral William J. Crowe and General David Jones), and current high-ranking officers as well, urged restraint; they held out for continued attempts to reason with Saddam Hussein. Indeed the November 29, 1990, *New York Times* reported that "In recent weeks, Gen. H. Norman Schwarzkopf . . . and Gen. Alfred Gray, the Marine Corps Commandant, have urged that the United States avoid a rush toward war and give economic sanctions more time to work."[56] Whether the Iraqi leader would eventually have been thus persuaded will forever be unknown; with the luxury of retrospect it seems, so far, that sanctions may have had little impact upon him.

On November 29, 1990, the lead editorial of the *New York Times* was headed, "Once Again: What's the Rush?" Later its December 16, 1990, lead editorial was headed, "War by Default," and it warned that "the clock ticks down on President Bush's Jan. 15 deadline for war with Iraq—too fast." To many, including former Defense Secretary James Schlesinger and five other former secretaries of defense, not enough patience and restraint were being shown in the White House. It might fairly be said in any case that during the short time that did remain before a hot war began, President Bush's public posturing and name-calling of the Iraqi president did little to create a climate of trust or communication. Apart from the posturing and bravado of the Iraqi leader, the case could even be made that his U.S. counterpart showed few signs of willingness to enter sincerely into a problem-solving negotiating session with a man whom he characterized as "an Arab Hitler."

As to the discrimination principle (not attacking civilians, but rather combatants only), the controversial aspects of the Gulf War were the question of whether or not the bombing was indeed "precision," the bombing of the civilian infrastructure, and the postwar sanctions (which punish the weakest members of the Iraq society, as indicated above). After the cease-fire, General Merrill McPeak, Air Force chief of staff, disclosed that Iraq and occupied Kuwait had been hit by 88,500 tons of bombs. Of this number only 7 percent (6,520 tons) were the "smart" bombs shown to the U.S. public via television by military-approved sources. About 90 percent of this 7 percent hit their targets smartly. The remaining 93 percent (81,980 tons) were "dumb" bombs. Three-quarters of these missed their targets, yielding an overall accuracy figure of only 30 percent.[57] The film footage shown to the U.S. public was misleading in that it implied much greater discrimination in hitting military targets than was actually the case, and it was misleading also insofar as the ostensible bombing accuracy was used in rhetoric to buttress the administration's claims to be waging a just war.

The greatest concern in the U.S. arose after the mid-February bombing raids against electrical power, sewage, and water services in Iraq. Although one could argue that disrupting a country's civilian base could weaken its overall war-fighting capability, this strategy is precisely what the just war theory has defined as immoral. Similarly with postwar sanctions: sanctions, or embargoes, notoriously afflict the weakest parts of a nation—its aged, children, poor, and sick. As just war theoretician Michael Walzer has argued, sanctions are merely a return to the siege approach to warfare, which is a direct attack upon civilians. This is proscribed by just war thinking.[58]

The proportionality principle states that the achieved good in war should outweigh the harm done in the process. Here the controversy has centered upon the "turkey shoot" of retreating—or was it withdrawing?—Iraqi soldiers on the "highway of death," or "highway to hell," as the Jahra Road from north of Kuwait City to Basra came to be known. Although the U.S. president's press secretary announced on February 23, 1991, that *withdrawing* Iraqi forces (from Kuwait) would not be attacked, three days later President Bush said, "He is not withdrawing. His defeated troops are retreating."[59] The distinction is crucial, because *retreating* soldiers could be attacked. In any event, U.S. army estimates are that on this road 25,000 Iraqi soldiers and 4,000 of Iraq's 4,200 tanks were destroyed in a "target-rich environment."[60] Critics of this action point out that according to military ethics, an enemy should be given a chance to surrender; this was not afforded, they say, the helpless Iraqi soldiers, who were instead simply massacred.

There is a difference in just war thinking between the issues of whether or not to enter a war, and the right way(s) to fight it once it is underway. Whether the U.S. was correct to enter this war, or whether our timing was appropriate, is still a matter of considerable debate today. Whether the war was fought largely, completely, or not at all in a moral way is also a frequently debated question—at least in some circles. Perhaps further reflection would prompt the thought that we should not expect that a war will be fought morally, once underway. This is because in war there is the paramount need to give one's own fighting personnel the greatest possible support, almost without consideration of ethics and morality; and it is because of issues of overwhelming savagery in personal combat—psychological matters as familiar as the *Iliad*'s timeless recounting.

But all these things, if true, place even greater importance and urgency upon rightly using alternative means to solving international disputes in the first place. Professor Elshtain, in looking to the war's destructive potential and the need for massive help to clean up and rebuild afterward, remarks, "Just war argument precludes a punitive peace. . . . The war did not dislodge [Saddam Hussein]. A just peace must not try to do so over the malnourished bodies of Iraqi children."[61]

Much, though not all, of the Christian leadership in our country and elsewhere did not regard the Gulf War as just. Instead high-level church statements were persistently critical. The president-bishop of the Episcopal Church in Jerusalem and the Middle East, for instance, released "A Message for Peace" on August 21, 1990, blasting all who prepared for war.[62] On October 5, 1990, Presiding Bishop Edmond Browning of the Episcopal Church in the U.S.A. spoke to all Episcopalians, calling for restraint on the use of force and on the tendency to demonize others; he also urged the avoidance of war as a means to rectify our differences with the Iraqi leader.[63] On November 15 the National Council of Churches condemned U.S. policy in the Gulf and called for an immediate withdrawal of most U.S. forces in the region. The N.C.C. criticized the U.S. administration for its "reckless rhetoric," "imprudent behavior," and its aggressive military buildup. It charged that "rationales offered for the steady expansion of U.S. presence have often been misleading and sometimes even contradictory."[64] Similarly the National Conference of Catholic Bishops on November 12 sent a letter to the U.S. administration criticizing the Gulf buildup.[65]

If there was a problem with church-based criticism of the war, or with the church's need to counter a politically self-serving misappropriation of just war theory, it may have been that church teaching was not energetically appropriated at the local level. Maybe applying a careful critique at the time was beyond either the intellectual capacity or the courage of local clergy and lay leaders. After all, the war was popular, once it got underway, and most Americans wanted it over with, with as little trouble to them as possible. But in fact there remains the devastation to Iraq resulting from the war, and the additional deaths and destruction befalling Kurds and Shi'ites immediately afterward—these were people encouraged by the U.S. president to overthrow Saddam Hussein, and they inferred a promise of support that, however, never came. And there remain today more than 2 million refugees and displaced persons.

ANY LESSONS FOR CHRISTIAN LEADERS?

In this amiable land we may or may not be conscious of what a luxury it is that life simply goes on. It is easy to forget those other people in Iraq, and their devastation, for which we do bear considerable responsibility. A church is the right place to remember what we have wrought, and that ethics and morality are concerned with faithfulness to God in Christ, and with being a holy and peaceable people. National level Christian leadership was as forceful and informed as one could reasonably want, but something seems to have failed dreadfully at the local level, where the clergy and lay leaders, and the people, are.

We need leadership people in the secular world and in the church who are acutely conscious of our war addiction and the satanic power of nationalism. We need Christian women and men who dare to look at any project holding such destructive power, and analyze it from the standpoint of its potential victims. We need to reappropriate the language of character, recovering it from military nuance, and casting it in the context of Christian peacemaking. We need to know that that spirituality is false which only drugs or diverts us from the struggles for peace; we have to see that during a time of war fever, and the stakes will be infinite for war's victims, spirituality can only mean lucidity, the antidote to bad faith.

We need to live our lives fully grounded in the love of Christ, lest we be swept away by governmental lies, hypocrisy, and propaganda. We need to have the courage to recognize that, yes, OUR government is not essentially virtuous or even benign, but that it is immensely capable of bringing enormous destruction to others. We need to study what causes war and what causes people to support it, and study what good outcomes allegedly result from it; we need to study who gains from war, and where the monies flow and who gets rich from it. We need to see clearly that appeal by any leader—Christian or not—to "just war" theory is a lie in this age of horrendous and indiscriminate weaponry. We need leaders who will wake up and come to a spiritual, moral, and theological honesty concerning the elemental and abiding truth that Jesus Christ never, not once, even hinted that any of us should cause anybody else to be killed in war or in any other way.

In short, when it comes to war fever, we need Christian leaders who are Christian.

DISCUSSION QUESTIONS

1. What are your exact feelings when a national leader urges war?
2. Would you want your children in the armed forces during a time of war?
3. Do you differentiate between the political and military leaders of an enemy nation and the civilian population of the same?
4. Does the church have any rightful role to play when a country's political leaders mobilize for war? If yes, what is it?
5. Would U.S. military involvement in distant places be less likely if our military budget were similar to, say, Australia's?
6. Is "high-tech" weaponry *good?* Why or why not?
7. Who benefits from wars? Who "loses"?
8. What is the national policy that governs when and where we become involved in a war?

SOCIETAL INTEGRITY
AND OFFICIAL DECEIT

I grew up in a little village in upstate central New York and did the usual things children my age did, including visit the shoe store in Syracuse. The best part of that was putting my feet inside a machine that enabled me to see through the new shoes into the feet inside them, and indeed through the feet to the bones. I could wiggle my feet and see them move inside the shoe; it was a bit like looking at your bare feet in shallow water. About the same time I wore an inexpensive wristwatch with numbers on it that glowed in the dark. I believed I could "recharge" the glowing numbers by holding the watch close to a light or leaving it in the sun. I also remember wearing it every day and every night—especially at night.

I was too young to think further about the shoe-store machine or the radium dial wristwatch until several years later when I ran into an old friend from high school. We had a wonderful reunion, which he had to cut short for a doctor's appointment. He had suffered with adolescent acne, he explained, and his parents had had his face treated with radiation. These days he has to be checked regularly for complications from the radiation.

I also remember working for a major defense contractor during the summers between college years, and analyzing bomb-blast data coming from some island in the Pacific. The dominant thought I had at the time, accompanied by a certain exhilaration, was that I was cleared to read documents stamped "secret." To be on the inside of secrecy, especially official secrecy, was mildly intoxicating to my adolescent mind. No doubts about the blasts themselves, or the purpose, potential applications, or effects of such things bothered me. Lots of people didn't know what was dangerous in those days, or why. There was a rather general trust in the intelligence and diligence of our leaders—in both industry and government—that today seems charming.

But today there is a sea change in public confidence. This has to do with a widespread fear, pessimism, fatalism, cynicism, or mistrust concerning things that emit radiation and what they do to people. Concern is evident, too, regarding the people who are supposed to be protecting us from the radiating things, and the degree of honesty, professional integrity, and diligence they have or do not have. The enormous magnitude of nuclear energy in any form makes urgent the question, What kinds of people are presuming to control the radiating things, and can the rest of us trust them? This is the leadership question, par excellence, from an ethics point of view— and it prompts the question of what kind of alternative leadership should we seek in the struggle for accountability, honesty, and public safety.

The eminent M.I.T. scientist Norbert Wiener decided to cease working on military-weapons projects, explaining, "I don't give four-year-olds razor blades." One assumes that instead of disparaging the military, Wiener was saying that because of the destruction they cause, nuclear weapons have now overwhelmed any reasonable confidence we might have in the imperfect human beings who are supposed to control them. Interestingly, a growing number of people apply Wiener's analysis to nuclear-power generation, notably after Three Mile Island and especially after Chernobyl. As more comes to light about nuclear-weapons manufacture, the application is being made to that as well. Chernobyl, however, stands as the summary symbol of all our fears concerning radiation and our real or imagined susceptibility to danger from nuclear energy or weapons production. Chernobyl indeed represents the crystallization of everyday fears of human error and incompetence, of industry and governmental secrecy and deceit.

Certainly there are many people presently benefitting from nuclear power, many who benefit directly from jobs in nuclear-weapons production, and there are many who have no concern about nuclear safety in any of its aspects. Further, there are reams upon reams of paper documenting the hours, days, and years of safe nuclear energy and materials production in our country and elsewhere. Whether or not nuclear energy or weapons are good things overall is not under consideration here. Rather, the focus is upon certain ethical issues arising for all of us with respect to secrecy, deceit, and perhaps contempt of the public on the part of certain leaders, because in industry and government certain misdeeds of a characterological sort have provoked the skepticism and mistrust of ordinary citizens. Christians need to insist upon leadership that places highest priority upon the integrity of society—that is, upon the integrated communality and sociality which makes openness, trust, truthfulness, and respect the assumption and reality of public life and discourse. (The razor blades' inherent danger I leave to the analysis of scientists and technologists; moral questions concerning *some* of those who play with them are of interest just now.)

The gun lobby frequently announces that "Guns don't kill. People do." Their endeavor is to remove the emphasis from the supposedly neutral technology and shift it to its users. Some proponents of nuclear power and weapons production make the identical case. An ethical inquiry is designed to explore the "people" aspect of nuclear technologies; in its concern with public welfare, the ethics focus is upon such familiar vices as negligence, lying, self-serving secrecy, incompetence, deliberate obfuscation, and the like. When practiced against the public, behaviors of this sort neither inform nor make for a secure citizenry; they are not coherent with the communality and sociality of the biblical notion of justice. Moreover, according to common morality they can plainly be wrong.

■   ■   ■

CHERNOBYL AS GOLEM

The responsibilities of leaders in any field to the larger society tend to be specified by the perceived needs of that society. When it understands itself as a justice type of community, a society's own sense of its "need to know" places some obligation upon its leaders to provide the people with relevant, truthful information. What is the American public's attitude toward nuclear technologies—particularly since Chernobyl? There is a general skepticism concerning the impact of any technology upon us. A National Science Foundation survey conducted in 1987 said that people believe science and technology will negatively affect "people's moral values." Another study found that 42 percent of all Americans believe that technological advance in general should be inhibited to "protect the overall safety of our society"—according to the U.S. Congress's Office of Technology Assessment.[1]

The well-publicized mistakes, the grudgingly publicized mistakes, and the near mistakes at nuclear-power and weapons-production installations around the world have planted fears in the minds of millions of people. To rational fears are added irrational ones, fed by ignorance of what radiation does. Chernobyl in particular symbolizes many of the things of which people are afraid; indeed it is regarded by many as the most destructive accident ever caused by humans. Chernobyl's impact upon the human psyche is difficult to assess, except possibly by the use of the golem, part of medieval Jewish folklore. The golem was a technologically created figure magically brought to life. It did precisely what—to speak anachronistically—it was programmed to do; and lacking any capacity to do otherwise, it frequently crashed forward on its unswerving way, creating enormous destruction.

Perhaps a modern-day golem can be found in the recent translation of Grigori Medvedev's book on Chernobyl. In it the author said this: "Meanwhile, the reactor was burning away. The graphite was burning, belching into the sky millions of curies of radioactivity. However, the reactor was not all that was finished. An abscess, long hidden within our society, had just burst: the abscess of complacency and self-flattery, of corruption and protectionism, of narrow-mindedness and self-serving privilege. Now, as it rotted, the corpse of a bygone age—the age of lies and spiritual decay—filled the air with the stench of radiation."[2] In its May 5, 1991, issue The *New Yorker* editorialized, ". . . the world does seem poised on the verge of a new era, and there may be no issue that more clearly defines the character of that era than how we as a species choose to deal with the technology represented by the charred Chernobyl reactor—a twisted hulk that will remain intensely radioactive for hundreds of years."

In all likelihood the American public is not well informed about what happened at Chernobyl. Nor is a Chernobyl event likely to occur in the U.S.—according to certain industry and government leaders! But nonetheless, the most dreaded unknown risks for Americans, according to the third edition of *The Emergency Public Relations Manual*, are nuclear-reactor accidents, nuclear-weapons fallout, and radioactive waste.[3] Some of these fears, and certain of their causes, warrant the attention of those who minister to people and feel a responsibility for the larger public welfare. From an ethics standpoint, what are some of the problematic issues?

■ ■ ■

NEGLIGENCE

Media reports convey descriptions of negligence: "Almost five years after the Chernobyl nuclear disaster, the Soviet prosecutor general conceded today that there had been gross failures in the Government's cleanup plan and said some officials would face criminal charges for failing to protect the public properly from fallout and continuing radiation contamination." The *New York Times* story added that some officials responsible for the cleanup had not evacuated nearby people as safely and quickly as needed, nor had they heeded warnings of dangerously high radiation levels, nor had they buried radioactive wastes carefully, nor had they prohibited the construction of resettlement buildings in "contaminated regions." Moreover, cleanup workers were exposed to dangerous levels of radiation, and local farms continued to produce goods affected by the radiation.[4] A Soviet paper reported that over 23,000 officials involved in monitoring radiation following the Chernobyl explosion have been fined for negligence, and 5,500 have been fired.[5]

Grigori Medvedev was the deputy director of the Soviet Ministry of Energy responsible for nuclear plant construction at the time of the Chernobyl explosion. He has listed twelve U.S. nuclear power-plant accidents and eleven Soviet accidents—all due to negligence—that he feels are "precursors of the disaster." At Chernobyl itself the problems ranged from shoddy reactor design to poorly trained operating personnel, to the "delusion" and "arrogance" of the senior operators, to failure to issue adequate warnings following the explosion. (The day after the explosion very high levels of radiation could have been monitored in nearby Pripyat, but weren't, while children went to school, athletic events took place, and sixteen couples were married on schedule.)[6]

Near the end of his book Medvedev quotes American scientist Karl Z. Morgan with approval: "I would like to register a strong complaint regarding a practice that has developed in the nuclear energy industry, of 'burning' and even 'burning out' temporary employees. By this we mean employing poorly instructed and untrained persons temporarily to carry out 'hot' jobs." Morgan says that such employees are not likely to be aware of radiation dangers to themselves and others, and continues, "I consider the practice of burning out employees to be highly immoral and unless the nuclear energy industry desists from such practices, I (and I am afraid many others) will cease to be strong supporters of this industry. . . ."[7]

Because of notorious difficulties in evacuating large numbers of people from near a nuclear accident site, there is much skepticism about any sort of evacuation at all. Valery Legasov, the leader of the Soviet delegation to the August 1986 Vienna conference on assessing the Chernobyl explosion, said that due to the pattern of radiation spreading from the plant, "not a single one of our previously prepared emergency plans could be implemented."[8] Closer to home, Steve Comley, the owner of the Seaview Nursing Home, near the Seabrook nuclear power station in Massachusetts, asked the Nuclear Regulatory Commission (NRC) for their plan for how his elderly clients could be protected in case of a nuclear accident. He was told that if the patients could not be moved, they should receive potassium iodine, which would help block the intake of radiation to the thyroid. This, however, would not guarantee prevention from exposure, possible illness, or even death. In other words, there are no effective plans to protect people from a serious accident.[9]

Another aspect of negligence is overall operator incompetence. Chernobyl demonstrated the hazards of "people mucking around in a nuclear reactor, but not knowing the what and the why of safety systems and the limits of the reactor"—according to a NRC engineer at the 1986 Vienna conference.[10] In the U.S., thirty miles north of Baltimore, operator negligence in March 1987 caused the Peach Bottom plant in Pennsylvania to be shut down. The operators there had been cautioned that their diligence was crucial in running an old plant safely, yet federal regulators found the operators asleep in the control room.[11]

Concerns about negligence in nuclear-power generation are of a piece with concerns over negligence in nuclear-weapons production. There are fourteen military nuclear facilities in the U.S., each under the control of the Department of Energy. Many of these were built over thirty years ago and may be nearing the end of their productive lives. To the public, civilian or military nuclear plants constitute a worry. The fear is with anything emitting radiation. The prospect of negligence in managing facilities is therefore a serious matter. The Westinghouse Corporation, for instance, admitted in November 1988 to being "guilty of some of the same managerial lapses as its predecessors." Westinghouse was hired by the government to correct an ongoing situation at the Savannah River plant near Aiken, South Carolina. Savannah had recently incurred over thirty citations for reactor accidents and safety violations of various types. Westinghouse also admitted management problems at the Hanford Reservation near Richland, Washington, and at the Fernald, Ohio, Feed Materials Production Center.[12]

At Hanford there was a formidable legacy of negligence: "airborne radioactive particle emissions, at the rate of more than seven billion a month, were discovered at two main nuclear processing areas in 1947 and persisted for several years." This depressing story was followed by a statement by the chief Energy Department official at Hanford that "There is no reason to expect observable health impacts" from the releases. Hanford personnel conceded under questioning that no attempt had been made to discover harm. By July 12, 1990, an investigatory panel concluded that in the 1945–47 period, 5 percent of Hanford's 270,000 neighbors received airborne radiation amounts 1,200 higher than safe levels as judged by current standards.[13]

Negligent management was seemingly ubiquitous in the nation's nuclear weapons complex. At Fernald, Ohio, company employees had deliberately released radon gas on one occasion, and had released a uranium-bearing gas on a different one. A $78 million settlement was finally reached in June 1989 between the Energy Department and Fernald area residents. During the plant's thirty-five-year history, an amount ranging from half a million to 3 million pounds of uranium dust were released into the atmosphere.[14] Other health issues have been raised elsewhere, notably at the Rocky Flats, Colorado, nuclear-weapons facility and in the area of St. George, Utah.[15] At Rocky Flats on June 6, 1989, some seventy-five F.B.I. agents, operating under the code name Operation Desert Glow, carefully searched for instances of deliberate violation of environmental laws. This was the first criminal investigation of any of the military-weapons installations. A month after the raid, Energy Department officials discovered ten radiation safety problems during a week-long inspection, "including one involving leaking boxes of radioactive waste." Shortly after that the discovery of plutonium in plant ventilation pipes was announced—in spite of earlier denials by plant managers that it was there.[16]

Negligent regulation of negligent industry management is a type of compound problem. The then U.S. Energy Secretary, James Watkins, startled many when after assuming office he said in June 1989: "A culture of mismanagement and ineptitude will have to be overcome in [this] department before the nation's troubled nuclear weapons manufacturing plants can be brought into compliance with environmental and health laws." Commentators wonder whether Admiral Watkins's reforms will be able to make their way through the middle and lower levels of the Energy Department's bureaucracy.[17]

Perhaps the most pointed instance of public anger over negligent management occurred during the Three Mile Island (TMI) accident near Harrisburg, Pennsylvania, in 1979. When little was known by anyone about the problem, or the risks, a single NRC official initially advised an urgent evacuation of area residents. Since he had acted without the consent of his superiors, however, this was withdrawn. Governor Richard Thornburgh tried to get confirmation of the advisory, but was unsuccessful. During the first several hours, plant operators were unable to give either NRC officials or the press a clear statement. Subsequently TMI's officials told an exasperated public that the press had done a poor job of conveying information. The information problem continues to plague the nuclear-power industry. As recently as October 1990 the Department of Public Health in Massachusetts published a study indicating an adult cancer risk at the Pilgrim Nuclear Power Station, near Plymouth, four times higher than expected.[18]

Negligence and rumors of negligence continue to plague the operators and regulators of civilian and military nuclear installations. Public unease and mistrust are the results.

■   ■   ■

LYING

Lying by officials in industry and government is another factor in public concern over nuclear affairs. Again we are instructed by the Chernobyl experience. In the aftermath of public confusion upon the heels of official deception, Soviet physicians have used the term "radiophobia" to describe a new and pervasive psychological phenomenon. They defined the term in *Pravda* as "an increased psychoemotional reaction to a real or imagined danger of radiation."[19] Such a disorder is understandable in the U.S.S.R., following the Chernobyl explosion; it is understandable in the U.S., too, in the wake of the TMI accident. Radiophobia is increasingly likely to be manifested in the public sphere as more and more information comes to light concerning past instances of official lying. If radiation is not dangerous, why have we been lied to about it?

Thoughtful scientists recognize the importance of truth-telling in the matter of nuclear radiation. The chair of the National Research Council Committee on Risk Perception and Communication writes, "Communicators must be honest. Credibility is strengthened by honesty and lost by lying. But between these two ends of the spectrum lie persuasion, manipulation, and deceit." He recognizes the complexity of presenting truthful information of a highly technical nature to the public ("radiation adds to the problem of widespread public dread"), but he concludes that government agencies "must use competent and honest representatives and should enter into dialogue early with the interested and affected public."[20]

The most serious nuclear accident in the U.S. is the 1979 Three Mile Island incident. Here reports of radiation leak rates were found to have been falsified, apparently in a minimizing fashion, before the accident. After the accident, "the plant's owners repeatedly lied about the extent of the damage."[21] During the time when the unit was out of control an instrument technician came from TMI Unit 2, shouting, "Christ! The core is melting!" This verified the feelings of others. "But for two days officials of General Public Utilities, which owns TMI, did not tell the public what they knew."[22] Thus before, during, and after the most dangerous nuclear event in our nation's history, officials were caught lying. Given that 26,000 known nuclear "mishaps" have occurred in the decade since TMI in the U.S., and that the Nuclear Regulatory Commission assigns a 40 percent probability to another meltdown in the next twenty years, the public's concerns about radiation and lying seem warranted.[23]

The picture does not get much clearer several years after TMI. In September 1990, for example, two health studies appeared to minimize the health risks from TMI radiation. "No convincing evidence" is to be found in cancer incidence rates around the Harrisburg plant, proclaimed one study. Another study, by the National Cancer Institute (NCI), examined cancer deaths in counties surrounding nuclear-weapons facilities and nuclear power plants. It purported to find "no increased risk of death from cancer" in those areas. Although initially reassuring, both studies were criticized, even by their sponsors. The prestigious *New England Journal of Medicine* rejected the TMI study as "inconclusive." The citizens' organization TMI Alert found it "flawed and misleading," ignoring "serious adverse health effects." The study's researchers failed to interview people living in cancer-cluster areas downwind of the installation during the accident. The higher rates of lung and blood cancer close to the plant were dismissed as due to "smoking and chance." That the study turned up no increase in breast or thyroid cancers was criticized because these usually develop after a longer time lapse, perhaps thirty years. The NCI study was criticized for diluting the cancer incidence by examining countywide figures, rather than looking closely at downwind incidence; nor did the NCI investigators attempt to contact former nearby residents who had since moved away.[24]

Methodologically flawed studies do not establish the charge of lying. They do, however, mislead and can be used by anyone who intends to deceive. In considering this sort of problem, one government official says, "Problems arise when issues such as epidemiological studies or their implications are complex. When such studies are summarized for the public, persuasion techniques are often employed—highlighting selected facts, framing the way facts are presented, or appealing to authority or emotion." We are no longer surprised at such political uses of data: "Public and private advocacy groups are expected to use such techniques," but their use by governmental officials in a democracy is highly questionable.[25]

Lying by high government officials not only affects their credibility with U.S. citizens; it also angers and confuses others. For instance on December 5, 1965, the U.S. aircraft carrier *Ticonderoga* was returning from a bombing mission in Vietnam to the U.S. Navy base at Yokosuka, Japan. Its logs stated it was seventy miles from Japan's Ryukyu Islands when an A-4 airplane, with a nuclear bomb on board, rolled off an elevator and disappeared into the sea. Pilot, plane, and bomb were lost. A Defense Department news release in 1981 said, "The incident occurred more than 500 miles from land"— referring to China. William M. Arkin and Joshua M. Handler investigated the incident and verified in 1989 that the *Ticonderoga* was indeed seventy miles from the Japanese islands; they questioned the veracity of the news release. A Pentagon spokesman replied that the bomb was 500 miles from the Asian mainland; he added that the Japanese island was anyway "a very small island in that chain."[26]

The Japanese government began to question the U.S. government, which then responded, in part: "The nuclear device involved . . . was not designed to remain . . . intact at extreme ocean depths; therefore structural failure occurred before it reached the ocean floor . . ." The idea was that seawater rushed into the "high explosive compartment" and that therefore "no nuclear . . . detonation can ever occur in the environment now or in the future." Further, regarding its environmental impact, said the Pentagon, tests indicated that "the involved nuclear material" will soon dissolve in seawater; "Therefore, there is no environmental impact." The Japanese government, sensitive to nuclear matters, and sensitive to its relationship with the U.S., chose to accept the Pentagon statement. Arkin and Handler summarize: "The recent uproar in Japan over the hydrogen bomb lying near the Ryukyus," and other events including the Navy's "neither-confirm-nor-deny" position on shipboard nuclear weapons, "will continue to provoke worldwide concern." The authors state, "A fuller airing of nuclear accidents, the outcome of nuclear testing and research, the nature of nuclear diplomacy, the details of nuclear strategies, and the extent to which nuclear waste and residue has been strewn over the globe is already shifting public opinion about continuing the nuclear era."[27]

Lying raises numerous questions about the intentions of other people. When those others have access to things emitting radiation, public confidence and our overall sense of security is undermined, at best. At worst, we become deeply suspicious; this is not the stuff of human community.

■   ■   ■

GOVERNMENTAL SECRECY, DENIAL, AND COVER-UPS

Many U.S. advocates of nuclear power and weapons production have tried to place an infinite distance between the Chernobyl event and any possible parallel in our nation. Certain elements of human conduct are similar in each place, however, including governmental obfuscation which is on the historical record. For instance, Zhores A. Medvedev (no relation to Grigori), reporting on the 1987 trial of high-level Chernobyl managers, disclosed that in 1983 the installation's power-station director had certified the reactor as working properly, even though there had not been a careful check of the safety systems.[28] This deceit was probably practiced upon the official's hierarchs within the Soviet system. The system itself had been pervaded with secrecy, however, for like that in the U.S., the Soviet nuclear-power industry "had its origins in, and still has links to, the nuclear-weapons program."[29] As will be shown below, the origin of the U.S. nuclear program has also been shrouded in official secrecy from its World War II beginnings; this has resulted in a history of secrecy and deceit in our country.

Perhaps the primary building block in the structured secrecy of nuclear affairs is the tendency of individuals to keep troubling data even from themselves. Grigori Medvedev's book contains a fascinating description of elemental human self-denial when a catastrophe unfolds: "In the first split second, you experience a feeling of numbness, of complete collapse within your chest and a cold wave of fright—the main reason being that you have been taken by surprise, and that . . . you have no idea what to do . . . while the needles of the automatic printer drums and the monitoring instruments are swinging in all directions. . . ." Simultaneously the mind frantically wrestles with the responsibility question: Who has done this?[30]

Testimony submitted to the Chernobyl inquiry by the shift foreman, Viktor Grigoryevich Smagin, describes the denial practiced by people confronted with massive evidence of the truth:

> I left the control room and hurried up the stair-elevator well to level +27 (89 feet). . . . On the way I bumped into Tolya Sitnikov, who looked really ill, his skin a dark brown from the nuclear tan. He could not stop vomiting. Making a big effort to overcome his nausea and weakness, he said, "I checked everything. . . . I was in the central hall, on the roof of V block. There's a lot of graphite and fuel up there. I looked down into the reactor. I think it's been destroyed. It's blazing away. . . ."
>
> The fact that he said "I think" says something of the torment Sitnikov was going through. Even he, a physicist, was unwilling

to believe the whole truth. What he had seen was so horrendous that he simply could not believe it himself.[31]

■　■　■

Psychological denial on the individual level during a crisis is understandable; we tend to accept it. Official denial after the crisis has begun is more calculated, and thus more open to criticism. John Ahearne writes of Chernobyl, "At first the Soviet government denied that an accident had occurred. By the time Soviet officials began to release information, varying accounts had already spread throughout Europe." The consequences of official denial were severe: "Lack of official information and poor explanations by local governments led to widespread confusion about human safety and the risk to crops, animals, and marketed foodstuffs."[32] Indeed, one of the first and most unfortunate aspects of official denials is that timely evacuations of nearby residents were not undertaken. What was saved in preventing early panic may well have been lost in subsequent health risks. Thus, four years after Chernobyl a Soviet delegation submitted an urgent request to the U.S. and the world in Washington for medical help. At a news conference at the Soviet embassy, a physician, Yuri Shcherbak, decried Soviet "government-imposed" secrecy while announcing a shortage of medical equipment, radiation detectors, and housing to deal with an enormous social problem. Shcherbak said, "Chernobyl is the gravest warning to all humankind; the warning that the development of super technology systems may lead to great damage and perhaps a threat to all living things on earth."[33] Perhaps most disheartening of all is the recent report that the Supreme Soviet's special commission investigating Chernobyl came across two top-level secret government orders: "One from 1987 classifying as secret any information on the extent of radiation contamination, and one from 1988 decreeing that no medical diagnosis may connect an illness with radiation exposure."[34]

In the U.S., where the prospect of lawsuits troubles our minds, there is an implicit incentive for governmental or industry spokespersons to deny or minimize possible dangers. "In a highly litigious society, legal staffs pressure agency officials or industry spokesmen to say as little as possible about hazards or accidents. Legal advisors warn officials that any explanation or statement of responsibility may be used later as the foundation for multimillion dollar lawsuits."[35]

One means to dissemble is by the manipulation of data. Certain forms of risk comparisons are employed to make public acceptance more likely. For example, "Supporters of nuclear plants often compare exposure to radioactive releases from normal operations with the risk of death from smoking, skiing, or getting chest x-rays."[36] The difficulty with these kinds of comparisons is that people may choose to avoid riskful behaviors, but they may be unable to avoid having a nuclear plant imposed upon their neighborhood. I have already mentioned the practice of selectively presenting and interpreting results from statistical or other studies. Still another instance of deceit is official cleaving to the comforting view that Chernobyl is not a warning we need to heed—whether the officials doing so are Soviet or U.S. Against this, Grigori Medvedev writes, "Chernobyl calls on us to use our reason and our analytical powers, so that we will not forget what happened, and will look clearly at our misfortune and avoid glossing over it."[37]

■   ■   ■

CHELYABINSK AND HANFORD

One nuclear accident in the Soviet Union closely parallels a U.S. situation—both in the technology of what occurred, and in the official secrecy used to cover it up. In 1979 Zhores A. Medvedev published his book, *Nuclear Disaster in the Urals*, which first opened Western eyes to a major accident that had been covered up by Soviet authorities since the late 1950s.[38] Chelyabinsk-40, a plutonium-manufacturing plant about ten miles east of the town of Kyshtym, had been built in the late 1940s. Some time between late 1957 and early 1958 an explosion of a radioactive waste dump occurred. This was precipitated, according to Medvedev, by gases in contact with the hot waste. The radioactivity spread around the nearby territory amounted to 20 million curies (according to Western estimates)—four times the Hiroshima amount. A similar, though smaller, event occurred at the Hanford Nuclear Reservation in Washington State. This resulted in the release of about 340,000 curies of iodine 131 into the atmosphere in 1945. The Hanford leak, however, was no accident; officials simply wanted to vent the waste in the easiest way.

Official secrecy surrounded both the Chelyabinsk and Hanford incidents. Soviet cover-ups of the Chelyabinsk accident continued until June 1989; the CIA kept silence on it as well. On June 16, 1989, Soviet officials finally admitted the truth concerning this thirty-two-year-old accident. Radioactive particles covered a 400 square mile area, and 10,000 people were forced to flee. "Thirty rural villages vanished from Soviet maps, fishing was banned in lakes, dams were built to contain radioactive waterways and rivers were diverted with canals, according to Western accounts." Tass indicated in 1989 that the area was able to resume its economic activity only in 1978, and then in only 80 percent of the radiated zone. "The remaining area was turned into a reserve."[39] But for many years there was no official acknowledgment that any such thing had happened. Eventually Herbert Scoville, chief of scientific intelligence for the CIA from 1955 to 1963, told CBS's "Sixty Minutes" on September 11, 1980, that both the Atomic Energy Commission and the CIA had known about the Chelyabinsk accident when it occurred. This information was kept secret from the American people presumably to avoid inflaming public skepticism about nuclear power.[40] Similarly, secrecy shrouded the Hanford release until 1986, when antinuclear activists "forced the release of nineteen thousand pages of government documents. . . ."[41]

A NEW CANDOR?

The *Los Angeles Times* reported in June 1989 that in the wake of criminal investigations into environmental and public-health concerns at the Rocky Flats, Colorado, nuclear-weapons plant, the Energy Department was going to end its policy of secrecy. In the same announcement, Deputy Energy Secretary Henson Moore declined comment, however, on specific charges of negligence in the plant's operation; so one wonders where the truth indeed lies. Moore did say, however, "These plants were built in the 1950s and the philosophy was this is a secret operation, not subject to any laws by the state." The general attitude, said Moore, was "just butt out."[42] Nearly two years later the same Energy Department, in a press release announcing a $241 million R and D budget request for nuclear-reactor development, omitted the word *nuclear* altogether from its 800-word statement—arguably a tactic to avoid public response by obscuring what it actually intended.[43] Despite its professed new policy of candor, the Energy Department's actions still appear designed to obscure its plans. Therefore the question arises, What is the record of secrecy as opposed to openness in the operation of governmental nuclear-weapons facilities? This can perhaps be considered by means of a listing of incidents at selected plants.

■ ■ ■

SECRECY AT HANFORD

Since 1943 the principal activity at this east-central Washington State facility has been large-scale manufacturing of weapons-grade plutonium. For a number of years in the mid to late 1940s, radioactive particles were emitted into the air at a rate exceeding 7 billion a month. Robert Alvarez, once known as the Atomic Energy Commission's "leading independent authority on the agency's health programs and environmental practices," has been outspoken in criticism of official secrecy. He and others hold that "the unwritten but persistent policy of the AEC and its successor, the Energy Department, has been to ignore, suppress, and publicly deny evidence of hazards. In this pattern science is not used to focus on problems but to cloud their appearance and allow agency officials to deny their existence."[44]

Critics point to the suppression of government emission measurement data for decades, with some 270,000 neighbors in a ten-county area around Hanford being exposed to radiation while being told nothing. When in 1986 information concerning the suppressed data came to light, the Energy Department denied that the released radiation could be responsible for illness. In July 1990 a prestigious panel of scientists announced that 13,700 people—approximately 5 percent of the overall population—had probably each absorbed the equivalent of 1,650 chest x-rays from 1944 through 1947, and that an unspecified number of children may have absorbed over eighty times this amount of radiation to the thyroid.[45]

Some of the staggering implications of this are sketched by Karen Dorn Steele, an investigative reporter for the Spokane, Washington, *Spokesman-Review.* She writes: "Most at risk are the 6,800 children, now 44–48 years old, who were born in Benton, Franklin, and Walla Walla counties in 1942–46." These were infants who may have absorbed enormous amounts of radiation to the thyroid from contaminated milk. If one estimates that 1 rad ("radiation absorbed dose") is equivalent to approximately fifty chest x-rays, these infants received the equivalent of over 145,000 chest x-rays in the thyroid. They also may have received 423 rad (approximately equivalent to 21,150 chest x-rays) from contaminated vegetables.[46]

Official secrecy concerning the Hanford leaks was supposed to be an item of the past. Yet on September 19, 1991, the investigative agency of the U.S. Congress, the General Accounting Office (GAO), reported that the Energy Department and its contractor, Westinghouse, "knew for months about a huge leak in a waste tank" at Hanford "but kept it secret, apparently in violation of Federal law." The waste tank had long been known to be leaking very radioactive wastes, with government estimates placing the total at around 5,000 gallons. But the GAO investigation revealed that both Westinghouse and the Energy Department "knew for months that the tank had leaked far larger amounts of contaminated water, perhaps 800,000 gallons, into the soil, but had kept it secret." Senator John Glenn, chair of the Senate Governmental Affairs Committee, remarked upon "a continuing pattern of behavior by the Department of Energy and its contractors to downplay the seriousness of its contamination problems at Hanford."[47]

SECRECY AT FERNALD

The uranium processing plant at Fernald, Ohio, on the Great Miami River near Cincinnati, is somewhat misleadingly known as "Feed Materials Production Center." When uranium oxide leaked into the local water supply, nearby residents began to question what was happening inside the plant. A class-action suit was filed in 1985 by over 14,000 Fernald residents against the NLO, Inc., firm that operated the plant at the time. In the aftermath of this suit, then Energy Secretary John S. Herrington conceded that for decades the Energy Department had been aware of releases of "thousands of tons of radioactive waste" into the Fernald environment. He also admitted that the Fernald plant had "ignored repeated warnings about the health and safety risks at the plant."[48] By 1990 the Energy Department had negotiated a settlement for $78 million, was facing a $1.6 billion lawsuit from employees charging exposure to radioactive particles, and had decided to keep the plant permanently closed.[49]

SECRECY AT SAVANNAH RIVER

In early 1988 a heretofore secret list was released of thirty serious mishaps occurring at the nuclear-weapons material plant at Savannah River, South Carolina. The time span for these incidents covered the thirty-seven years of the facility's operation. It had been compiled by DuPont company supervisors. Although showing no serious accident, the list disclosed several near accidents. Senator John Glenn complained about the list's having been kept secret, and said that neither DuPont nor the Energy Department had been "forthcoming." DuPont denied concealing information from the Energy Department, and the department announced that with the relaxing of Cold War tensions, it would relax security requirements somewhat.[50]

SECRECY AT ROCKY FLATS

In February 1990 Gregg Wilkinson, former chief of the Epidemiology Group at Los Alamos National Laboratory, disclosed that when he published a research paper establishing a link between radiation exposure among workers and cancer rates, he was told by a high-level governmental official, "We should not be publishing trying to please peer reviewers but to please the Department of Energy."[51] Some studies of Rocky Flats workers show increases in leukemia and lymphoma; 10,000 former plant employees are suing the Energy Department for radiation exposure, and 50,000 Denver neighbors within five miles of Rocky Flats are doing the same in a separate action.[52]

The above are but a few examples of secrecy and deceit practiced more or less continuously by an agency of the U.S. government against its own citizens. By the standards of ordinary morality this is a shocking and shabby record. It constitutes a serious erosion of democratic society, and it should arouse all who care about the public good.

■　■　■

A BRIEF EXCURSUS UPON THE ETHICS
OF LYING AND SECRECY

Lying, the intention to deceive by one's statement, is, as Aristotle put it, "mean and culpable."[53] We must be able to rely upon truth-telling, or else witness the erosion of trust essential to human community and to the humane functioning of society's institutions. The recent well-documented erosion of public trust in U.S. governmental institutions is perhaps traceable to our rejection of "paternalistic lying." This is self-serving lying by authorities, which is cloaked in the guise of altruism for the presumed benefit of others. "To act paternalistically is to guide and even coerce people in order to protect them and serve their best interests, as a father might his children," according to ethicist Sissela Bok.[54] Despite the fact that, as much history demonstrates, some folks like to be lied to in this way, many of us don't. Probably most who do such lying would not want to be deceived this way either.

In the early pages of her splendid book, *Secrets*, Professor Bok writes, "Secrecy is as indispensable to human beings as fire, and as greatly feared. Both enhance and protect life, yet both can stifle, lay waste, spread out of control. Both may be used to guard intimacy or to invade it, to nurture or to consume. And each can be turned against itself; barriers of secrecy are set up to guard against secret plots and surreptitious prying, just as fire is used to fight fire."[55] At the book's conclusion Bok writes of an "illusion," which is "the belief that . . . secrecy and controls are neutral, that they carry no risks of their own, no danger of damaging creativity, innovation, and research, no barriers to commerce, no dangers to judgment and to character, and no risks of encouraging official negligence and corruption."[56] The greatest risks of secrecy arise when it is hooked to the massive power of government.

Secrecy is dangerous because, among other things, it diminishes our capacity to make judgments by limiting our knowledge, and therefore our informed choice. It can corrupt the moral character and choice-making of those having access to secrets by habituating them to manipulation and exploitation of the ignorant. Secrecy also prevents those cloaked by it from receiving feedback that might otherwise help them in evaluating decisions already made, and it tends to remove accountability on the part of its practitioners for their decisions. Secrecy, moreover, by its nature is discriminatory; it gives greater knowledge, and probably control, to those possessing it than to those excluded by it—hence it implies inequality.

Many in high government positions gather to themselves the aura of importance, and perhaps of invincibility, by cultivating an atmosphere of secrecy. What used to be the *arcana ecclesiae* of the holy church has become the *arcana imperii* of the government, with its "mysteries of state."[57] But hocus-pocus is no more morally commendable in the state than it was in the church. Part of the shock coming from the televised broadcasts of governmental hearings is connected to people's dismay that their leaders are neither particularly superhuman nor demonstrably sacred. (Kurt Vonnegut is said to have warned us that the people running this country are the folks we went to high school with.)

"The esoteric rationale for government secrecy," writes Sissela Bok, rationalizes official state actions "that would be immoral for private individuals." The idea that government mystifiers want us to accept is that the state (and its various agents and institutions) is somehow above the reach of "ordinary moral deliberation" as this applies to plain old people like the rest of us. Bok shows the dangers of government secrecy: "The esoteric rationale for [the state's control of secrecy and openness] may . . . help subdue and overawe the inhabitants of a state." But being subdued and overawed is not appropriate to a democracy. A presumably free society of equals requires everyone's recognition that governments are engaged in secret endeavors all the time, and that much of the motive for such secrecy, despite official disclaimers to the contrary, is to shield those undertaking certain acts from responsibility for those acts.

Motives of secrecy also frequently include accomplishing one's purposes without hindrance from others more directly affected by the contemplated action—as in keeping secret from its neighbors the accidents at nuclear installations. Bok writes, "There should be a strong presumption against government control over secrecy because of the abuses it can conceal, the power governments exercise, and their special obligations of accountability." Therefore "every effort" must be made to keep governmental secrecy to an absolute minimum, and to force openness upon those who are in positions of public trust, who indeed are there, in a democracy, to serve the people.[58]

WHAT THEN?

I am a Christian in no small degree because the Easter story offers the possibility of hope. It announces that precisely from out of the depths of the deepest darkness, a light broke forth. From within the locked places of officially authorized and legitimated death, the power of life burst out: "He is risen." The steely, impervious, governmental monolith, fortified by morally ambiguous leadership and by our own indifference, ignorance, and learned helplessness, is not new to Christian understanding. It is as old as imperial Rome and as current as Washington, D.C.

Drawing upon the deepest resources of their heritage, Christians must dare to face up to the threats and disasters of life, and to the ambiguities of political and industry leadership—for the gospel has us standing with both feet on the earth, yet with a reckless hope in the sovereignty of good—a power from another order of reality altogether, not of this world. We cannot be focused upon these religious affirmations in an escapist way; we must recognize clearly that blind trust in leaders is unwise, while we get beyond our disillusionment and anger to an adult responsibility for fixing what's wrong. What can save us is God's gracious goodness, experienced as nurturance, protection, respect for all people and nature, and a holy hope for a more humane way of being in community with one another. For these moral, theological, and spiritual things to be shaped and applied effectively in this imperfect world, we also need leaders—in the church and in society—who embody them and persist tenaciously with them.

I am a feminist in the sense that I believe what we can do is desist from presumptuous, masculine exploitation and aggression—against one another in society and against nature. We can develop and nourish the qualities of community-based accountability and mutual respect, which will make lying to one another, and keeping secrets, and a domination and entitlement mentality no longer tolerable in human affairs. We can not any longer accept for ourselves a passive role in society; we must ourselves become leaders in the struggle for a just, inclusive, truly democratic society. We still have to persevere and force others to engage in the worthy endeavor to make communality and sociality real in our country.

For strength for this long journey, I think just now of the true leaders among us, morally and spiritually speaking, like Maya Angelou. She and so many other African-American women for generations had been prey to an apparently invincible, technologically enforced, masculine monolith, which was the institution of slavery and its helplessness-inducing legacy. In one of her books exploring this topic she reports her investigations into the "ignorance and gullibility," and plainly the felt helplessness of so many of her kind. She concludes, with a joyful and profound awe, that "Although separated from our languages, our families and customs, we had dared to continue to live. We had crossed the unknowable oceans in chains and had written its mystery into 'Deep River, my home is over Jordan.' Through the centuries of despair and dislocation, we had been creative, because we faced down death by daring to hope."[59] ✓ Our predicament in the face of today's government monolith is not nearly as precarious as hers, or her forebears'. We have much to learn from her, and our task, when you think of it, is a lot easier.

The historical reference reminds me too of U.S. historian Charles Beard, who was once asked what he had learned from a lifetime of historical study. His reply: "First, whom the gods would destroy they make mad with power; second, the mills of God grind slowly, yet they grind exceedingly small; third, the bee fertilizes the flower it robs; fourth, when it is dark enough you see the stars."[60] The task for all people of good will—scientists, technologists, and church people alike—is to find the path of hope by the light of the stars and walk it with all the sisters and the brothers. We seek this no less from our leaders, in church and in society at large.

DISCUSSION QUESTIONS

1. What is your own experience with radiation?
2. What are the changes, if any, in your own confidence that public officials tell the truth?
3. If you regard yourself as suspicious concerning official statements, do you regard official deceit as permissible, or should it be exposed and challenged?
4. Do government and industry have a duty to inform and protect citizens concerning radiation hazards? If this duty is not honored, what should be done?
5. Does the U.S. have a duty to protect the environment from radiation contamination? If yes, what is the basis for this duty?
6. Can optimistic predictions concerning future benefits of atomic energy be reconciled with the record of past negligence? With the record of past deceit?
7. Why do people lie? Why would we assume no further lies?
8. What is gained and lost by closing down nuclear-weapons production facilities, and by whom?

THE ARMS TRADE

Women and men who take seriously the humane sensibilities of Jesus the Christ have trouble accommodating the international arms trade. Certain moral concerns chafe. There is profiteering that benefits a few, and there is enormous destruction—by weapons directly, or economic neglect indirectly—of the poor (predominantly women, children, and the elderly) in weapons-buying countries of the "two-thirds world."

A key theological and moral premise is that, according to Christian teaching, all human life possesses dignity, as signified in the Genesis 1:26–28 text announcing that humankind are made in God's image. The Noah covenant, recorded in Genesis 9, reinforces the point, constituting the last "international" covenant, so to say, between God and all people; this is a divine plea for protection of the lives of all from the predation of the powerful.

Divine commitment particularly to the poor and vulnerable in society is notable throughout the Bible. The application especially to women and children in impoverished countries lavishly spending resources on arms purchase is obvious. These are all the more at risk due to the fact that most wars these days occur within, rather than between, countries; notoriously, civilian populations suffer most in wartime.

Justice is denied by the neglect of essential human services in poor countries, as economic resources are drained into expensive arms purchases. Peace is eroded because the mere ownership of weapons makes their use more likely. Destruction of property and of the environment is similarly predisposed. Moreover, when authoritarian governments are made more muscular by greater arms capacity, there may be an increased tendency to use force against the people themselves. (The next chapter will present personal testimony to this phenomenon in certain poor countries.)

■   ■   ■

The Episcopal Church has a long history of concern over the consequences of arms-producing nations developing, procuring, deploying, selling, and exporting military weapons of war. In 1978, the Lambeth Conference of Anglican bishops, many from poor countries, meeting in England, echoed this concern. The General Convention of the U.S. Episcopal Church, gathering the following year, adopted the entire Lambeth resolution on "War and Violence" from which this passage comes:

> There is a worldwide misdirection of scarce resources to armaments rather than human need . . . [We call Christian people everywhere] to protest in whatever way possible at the escalation of the sale of armaments of war by the producing nations to the developing and dependent nations, and to support with every effort all international proposals and conferences designed to place limitations on, or arrange reductions in, the armaments of war on the nations of the world.

Of primary concern is the danger of increased warfare now escalating around the world, fueled by the sale of conventional weapons by the United States and other nations to foreign countries. A Christian could easily conclude that the United States should neither export nor sell conventional arms and weapons, for this international trade has both raised and realized the risk and devastation of war in our post–Cold War and overmilitarized world. Because of the peace implications of God's merciful love, preeminently the divine commandment to love even one's enemies, this seems morally unacceptable by the gospel of Christ and, therefore, to the Christian conscience.

Evidence abounds, however, that U.S. trade in weapons is escalating. Indeed, the United States now sells more arms to regions of potential conflict than all other suppliers combined. For instance, in the three years since Iraq's invasion of Kuwait, more than $38 billion in arms has been sold to countries in the Middle East alone.[1] This has to be seen as a threat to world peace; ironically, the increased danger itself is used in U.S. political life as a rationale for maintaining a large, strong military establishment. The forces driving this ultimately destructive trade policy are strong and entrenched.

In a recent issue of *World Policy Journal*, it is estimated that by the mid-1990s the United States will be supplying 70 percent of the world's arms.[2] This role of primary-arms-supplier-to-the-world is unpleasant for some Christians to contemplate, especially when in a democracy all of us are at least remotely responsible.[3] The Center for Defense Information, in any event, reports that "There are 180 nations in the world and the U.S. regularly sells weapons to 142 of them." Fifty-nine of these have authoritarian governments, where the people have no freedom to change their leaders nonviolently. Several of these nations are "threatened" at any moment by insurgent movements within them, with the resulting governmental claim that weapons are needed to keep order. But to a Christian, resistance to oppressive government might seem better met by opening up government to democratizing influences than by further repression, backed by U.S.-manufactured arms.

THE INTERNATIONAL CONTEXT

As of 1992–93, the five permanent members of the U.N. (the U.S., Russia, China, Britain, and France) were responsible for 85 percent of all arms exports. Other leading exporters were Germany, Italy, Switzerland, Poland, and the former Czechoslovakia. These nations have been the sole exporters of the most technologically sophisticated and expensive weaponry. Thirty non-Western countries now have developed their own indigenous arms industries, mostly capable of more modest, light, conventional weaponry such as artillery, armored trucks, helicopters, machine guns, rifles, and ammunition. In 1988, non-Western suppliers accounted for 12 percent of all arms exports, and 10 percent in 1991.

Recent U.S. military action in Somalia has brought that small nation to public attention. Drought was proclaimed to be the cause of the Somalian tragedy, but the real difficulty, in the view of many, was years-long weapons sales to the various heavily armed camps there. Much responsibility is placed upon the Carter and Reagan administrations by Representative Howard Wolpe (D-MI), who has long fought military aid to that country. When in 1979 the Soviet

Union shifted its military support of Siad Barre to Ethiopia, the United States "propped up [that] incredibly repressive, corrupt regime."[4] The Somalian affair is replicated many times over in other corners of the world.

Illegal, covert arms sales are made to various buyers around the world from the United States. American-made semiautomatic pistols, rifles, revolvers, shotguns, and ammunition worth millions of dollars are being used in distant corners of the globe. I spoke recently with a high-ranking Coast Guard officer who personally had seen large quantities of U.S. weapons interdicted on waterways in and around the former Yugoslavia; these were being used by all sides in that dreadfully violent context. Further as an example, with other members of the Episcopal Church's Peace Commission I examined expended American-made tear-gas canisters in the Ahli-Arab Hospital in Gaza, an institution supported by the Episcopal Church.

After years of trailing the Soviet Union in arms exports, the United States has become, in the 1990s, the leading arms vendor in the world. Between 1988 and 1991, the U.S. sold one half of the arms bought in the Middle East ($36.5 of $73 billion). United States arms sales to the developing world set a then-record of $18.2 billion in 1990, and decreased to $14.2 billion in 1991, before the post–Persian Gulf War selling spree in 1992, when American sales skyrocketed.

During this time, Russia sold $2 billion in arms to Syria; France sold $680 million to Saudi Arabia. In the same eighteen-month span, U.S. sales to Saudi Arabia, Egypt, Israel, Turkey, Kuwait, the United Arab Emirate, Bahrain, Oman, and Morocco totalled $26.8 billion. Many of the weapons sold were among the most sophisticated available—combat fighters, air-to-air missiles, air-to-ground missiles, cluster bombs, and laser-guided bombs.

In an effort aggressively to market weapons, the U.S. now subsidizes exhibitions of U.S.-made weapons at trade shows around the world. High-ranking personnel from the Defense Department and Pentagon attend these bazaars to encourage the purchase of American-made weapons. I passed by one of these in Manila in the spring of 1993, while en route to the mountains of northern Luzon to inquire into the violence and intimidation of civilians by government soldiers, paramilitary forces, and the leftist "New People's Army."

Frequently sale of particular weapons and/or weapons technology is justified by appeal to the presumably socially useful function of "dual-use" technology. This means the presumed capability of certain equipment to be applied to civilian as well as military uses. Typically sales of such items as infra-red sensors and computers are thus warranted, for instance. But there is potential for harm even to our own country from these sales; dual-use technology had been shipped by U.S. firms to Saddam Hussein, and then was used against U.S. military personnel by the Iraqi military.

The relatively benign appearance of dual-use technology makes it potentially valuable as a basis for reestablishing support to arms industries; it appears to be a kind of economic middle way with at least quasi-civilian implications. But Seymour Melman, emeritus professor of industrial engineering at Columbia University, holds that justifying arms sales of this kind of technology as a socially beneficial way to strengthen our economy is dubious. Specifically, "The Clinton dual-use program will be like a halfway house for defense-dependent firms." The major difficulty is that, in Melman's view, "In the land of dual-use, the military side always gets first preference in terms of technology, people, and money."[5] Mainly, dual-use technology fails as an attempt to switch over U.S. weapons manufacturing to peacetime production; it is too flimsy a strategy.

At every turn, attempts to limit arms sales meet a constant refrain: "If we don't sell arms, someone else will." This lowest-common-denominator morality seldom persuades, however, and decidedly does not tend to make us feel good about ourselves if we care about peace with justice. For Christians, expediency-based profiteering is very difficult to square with the life and teachings of Jesus the Christ.

THE DOMESTIC CONTEXT

American defense industries, like all industries, seek to maintain high profits. Long dependent on the production of weapons, they tend to rely upon the international arms trade when the domestic military budget is being reduced and new weapons purchases are likely to decline even more in the future. But the problem with trying to switch dependence to foreign sales is that, in the words of expert Paul Warnke, "The U.S. defense budget has a value that's greater than most national economies, and these foreign arms sales are more like a placebo that keeps things going to pacify the industry." Such a strategy is shortsighted: "It just postpones the day when there will have to be a substantial downsizing of the defense industry."[6]

Coming to terms with the emerging reality is difficult, and breaking dependence upon foreign sales takes on the aspect of an addiction drama. For instance, then-Deputy Secretary of State Lawrence Eagleburger told American embassies in 1990 that, "It is the policy of the United States that our diplomatic posts abroad should support the marketing efforts of U.S. companies in the defense-trade arena as in all other spheres of commercial activity."[7] The Clinton administration continues the policy, and with no overarching Cold War context to rationalize this, profit-taking emerges as the sole motive. But an arms race does sometimes result from the sales themselves, as can be seen in the Middle East, and it is generated by U.S. competition with itself. Specifically, when huge sales of expensive F-15E fighter-bombers (each equipped with laser-guided bombs) are made to the Saudis, correspondingly large sales of aircraft, $2 billion worth, to Israel are predisposed.

American companies currently export 15 percent of all conventional weapons they build. This is likely to grow to 20–25 percent. At its present rate, exports' share will have risen at General Dynamics from 17 percent of its business in the mid-1980s to 50 percent in the mid-1990s, and at Martin Marietta from 8 percent in 1991 to 20 percent in 1994. Raytheon projects its expansion to foreign buyers from 20 to 40 percent between 1992 and 1997. Indeed, an Aerospace Industries Association speaker recently noted: "Exports are no longer just the icing on the cake. They are the cake."

As of this writing, President Clinton has not rescinded any weapons program originally rationalized by the Cold War. Even the enormously expensive and technologically suspect B-2 stealth bomber is still going forward. Moreover, Clinton has brought back from the grave the SSN-21 Seawolf attack submarine, a form of the F-14 Tomcat missile (the "Bombcat"), and the Marine Corps' V-22 tilt-rotor plane—all programs earlier terminated by President Bush.

Particularly worrisome is that increasingly, in a frantic search for sales, our weapons-manufacturing corporations sell blueprints, data, components, machine tools, and sometimes complete factories to buyers in other countries. The chief result is that many poor countries have themselves become weapons manufacturers and even exporters. Turkey, for instance, in 1987 manufactured the Lockheed F-16 Falcon, an advanced fighter plane; by 1991 it was selling advanced U.S.-design aircraft from its own factories to Egypt. Presently Turkey is building UH-60 Blackhawk helicopters, Multiple-Launch Rocket Systems, and Stinger antiaircraft missiles.[8] The diffusion of U.S. weapons know-how means that the most sophisticated such weapon we have, the M-1A1 Abrams tank, is built in Egypt. South Korea, whose near northern neighbor seems presently troublesome to us, is nearly ready to manufacture F-16 aircraft and UH-60 helicopters. These supplement earlier "technical data packages" to South Korea for 105-mm howitzers, 155-mm howitzers, 106-mm recoilless rifles, 90-mm recoilless rifles, 60-mm and 81-mm mortars, 8–inch projectiles, M-18A1 antipersonnel mines, and so on.[9] From the perspective of North Korea, however their leadership is characterized in the U.S. media, this build-up must be assumed to have a purpose; such is the stuff from which wars are made, and driving such stuff, usually, are weapons profits.

Taiwan, Argentina, Indonesia, and Singapore are yet other countries where U.S. military technological capability is being installed, with other deals in the works for such nations as Brazil, Chile, India, Malaysia, Pakistan, and Thailand. In 1989, the U.S. exported $11.7 billion in military technology to culminate a decade averaging $8.3 billion in such sales per year. Without much or any review, our government routinely licenses each of these transactions, usually by means of "coproduction agreements."

One result of this technology diffusion is that sophisticated weapons are sold to still other countries that our government does not want to have them, because they pose security or human-rights problems for the U.S. Thus the U.S. Office of Technology Assessment reported in *Global Arms Trade* (1991) that these technology exports have "contributed to the emergence of numerous centers of advanced defense industry" elsewhere in the world, and that "each new center is capable of transferring technology and selling weapons to additional countries."[10] Another result of this is that, with respect to dual-use technologies in particular, we may be selling off some of our best competitive advantage in international, and perhaps eventually our own domestic, civilian markets.

Ironically, these developments make it ever more difficult for international agencies to monitor or control the weapons trade. In purely commercial terms, this adds to the creation of long-term competitors for American industries, a condition that belies the notion that arms sales will save jobs beyond the short-term. Indeed, a likely interpretation of the phenomenon is that in reality it is driven by short-term gain and not another thing.

Of particular concern is the fact that American contractors provide arms to countries with histories of human-rights abuses. In the 1980s, according to State Department and CIA analyses, over one-half of U.S. weapons sold abroad went to authoritarian governments. During the Cold War, this was justified with my-enemy's-enemy-is-my-friend logic. More recently, relations with Kuwait, Saudi Arabia, and other oil-exporting nations were justified on the basis of retaining access to crucial resources such as oil. Other trading partners are retained because they offer favorable military access agreements in exchange for weapons.

It seems evident that efforts to reduce military forces in order to invest more resources in our domestic needs are doomed if we continue to supply the world with arms. A leading reason for this is that the proliferation of conventional weapons will predictably insure an increase in international violence and, therefore, justify the need for a larger American military establishment. We will need appropriate force to protect us from the increasingly dangerous forces "out there" that we ourselves have largely created.

There is a final factor: Proponents of the weapons trade portray the conflict between limitation and promotion of arms sales as "arms control vs. jobs." With defense budgets shrinking, exports are making up the shortfall for contractors who complain they would otherwise have to shut down production lines and lay off workers. A "Jobs Now" coalition of seven aerospace corporations and six labor unions has come into being, actively promoting foreign arms sales. This kind of strategy does tend to be successful in the short run; huge sales in the fall of 1992, for example, were a direct result of arms-industry lay-offs, recession, and the resulting intensified lobbying by the weapons industry.

More sound as a long-term strategy, however, would be a sincere commitment by industry, government, and local communities to economic conversion.[11] There is impressive warrant for believing in the success of conversion. Following World War II, defense spending had dropped from 40 to 6 percent of the gross national product. With the aid of dedicated, imaginative planning, particularly supported by the Marshall Plan and G.I. Bill, and with the unleashing of unprecedented consumer orders, a war economy successfully converted into a postwar boom. This experience shows that conversion can be accomplished, even though we have been in a Cold War economy for much longer than the Second World War's duration; what is needed is the necessary determination. Jobs are needed to make retraining feasible for at least 2 million soldiers and defense workers. Mass transit, alternative energy, and waste management are areas usually mentioned as needing infusions of human and material resources.

The immediate context for conceiving economic conversion is the end of the Cold War. Although General Colin Powell has warned Congress that the real problem for military planners is "the unknown"—and notoriously the unknown is infinite, with infinite implications for military budgeting—the essential truth is that today we have no enemy worthy of us. This is what offers the opportunity to begin a shift to a productive, peacetime economy, in which workers are employed to manufacture goods and services that will enhance the quality of civilian life for all. After all, it is now widely recognized that our major national concerns are the things that a major commitment to domestic priorities can ameliorate: joblessness, homelessness, illiteracy, drug abuse, crime, crumbling schools and infrastructure, and so on.

General Douglas MacArthur once noted that "it is part of the general pattern of misguided policy that our country is now geared to an arms industry which was bred in an artificially induced psychosis of war hysteria and nurtured upon an incessant propaganda of fear."[12] The presence of defense-industry contractors and/or military installations in nearly every congressional district in our country demonstrates the degree to which what President Eisenhower called "the military-industrial complex" has insinuated into the fabric of American life. It also shows why it is so hard to become disconnected from this tar baby in order to establish a new economic foundation.

The military-related jobs that currently do employ American workers, and for which they have been so carefully trained, are not easily abandoned, obviously. And yet if by careful planning these jobs can be turned to socially useful purposes, no longer dependent upon military money, our country would stand a better chance of improving the overall quality of life for all our people. Literacy rates, mortality and morbidity rates, the numbers of people receiving health insurance, and so forth, could easily be raised substantially. The figures are clear. Michael Renner of Worldwatch argues, for example, that "while $1 billion in 1981 dollars would have created 9,000 jobs in guided missile production or 14,000 jobs in military aircraft production, the same amount would have created 21,500 jobs in local mass transit industries, 16,500 in water and solid waste pollution control, and 63,000 in educational services."[13]

Economic conversion expressly means "political, economic and technical measures for assuring the orderly transformation of labor, machinery and other economic resources now being used for military purposes to alternative civilian uses."[14] The specifics of the conversion process include the mandatory creation of "alternative use committees" within each military production facility or laboratory. These groups would include both labor and management people who would specify civilian production that could appropriately be undertaken at the given installation.

According to the conversion process, government-funded technical assistance would be provided to local committees for help in materials, plant changeover to alternative production, and marketing. The government would have to give ample advance warning of intended expiration of military contracts. Required retraining programs, particularly for supervisors, would help facilitate smooth transitions to new production. Relocation planning and funding would be provided as indicated, with guarantees of income support for affected employees during the transition period. Throughout, local control of the conversion planning process would be maintained. (Every year a bill with these basic provisions is introduced in Congress; it has yet to gain the necessary votes for passage. The result is needless chaos and suffering by employees and local communities.)

In October 1993 Professor Seymour Melman told the National Commission for Economic Conversion and Disarmament that presently 2.7 million Americans are employed in weapons manufacture, and that about the same number could be employed in civilian sector work "if current [domestic] markets currently served by imports were served from U.S.-based production."[15] Since, as Daniel Smith of the Center for Defense Information points out, American weapons exports support only 328,000 jobs, there is a large unrealized job potential in economic conversion. Melman insists that Defense Department reductions are "economically viable *only* if they are done in the presence of conversion plans and a program schedule that features a dollar-for-dollar transfer from military programs to civilian projects."[16]

Bringing the destructive and wasteful foreign arms trade to heel is eminently doable; economic conversion is an essential and humane element along the way.

SUMMARY

Current trends in the international arms trade create two interlocking cycles: (1) a continuing escalation of foreign trade in arms that increases international destabilization and violence, while seemingly justifying our own military build-up in response, and (2) a self-perpetuating dependence upon increased arms sales sustains the habitually high profits of the weapons industry: the more sales, the greater dependence, and vice versa.

Although some in the U.S. will surely continue to derive riches from arms sales, foreign arms sales will probably provide job protection for most employees for no longer than the short-term. The effects of such sales upon international stability, however, are long-term and unforeseeable. In some countries, arms sales or arms purchases justify military and political excesses created by earlier weapons transfers; the current proliferation of weapons opens the way for a demand for even more sophisticated weaponry to counteract weapons that have meantime fallen into the hands of former allies, now enemies. The tension between the Saudis and Israelis, once allied against Iraq, illustrates this.

What to do? According to current laws, when the executive branch approves a transaction, Congress has thirty days to override it with a veto-proof resolution in the Senate and the House. No such congressional override, however, has ever occurred. The time constraint is one factor. Another is that the congressional vote approving an arms sale is often not recorded, so members of Congress can say or vote as they choose without having to take public responsibility for their position. Altogether, lobbying pressures on Congress have been remarkably effective in promoting this growing business.

As an alternative to the present practice, the executive and legislative branches of government could (1) enforce current laws—the Arms Export Control Act and the Foreign Assistance Act—which are routinely ignored; (2) expand Congress' thirty-day period for action to bar a weapons transfer to at least thirty-days "in session," thus allowing more time to consider the long-term consequences of each arms deal; and (3) end taxpayer and other government subsidies for arms bazaars.

With respect particularly to transfers of weapons technology, Michael Klare believes that Congress should be notified in advance of all coproduction and licensing agreements valued at over $1 million, making room for congressional veto where appropriate. The approval process should require an "impact statement" that responds to international security and U.S. economic considerations. There should be, further, a State Department office to supervise and track these transfers, and mandatory inspection of all foreign manufacturing using U.S. technology should be authorized to check improper applications to unapproved projects.[17]

On a wider scale, the United Nations Conventional Arms Transfer Register invites comprehensive reports of arms transfers by each government. Although solicitation of arms is not yet a part of this, public reporting might help in building a worldwide climate to reduce overall procurement and sales. Especially in the absence of Cold War justification for engorging dictators with arms, the United States could play an important leadership role in having procurement added to the Register, and generally in cooperating with its letter and spirit.

Further, our government could play a leadership role in the development of international codes aimed at limiting arms procurement and sales, and licensing for arms manufacture. Various concerns to be explored might be the belligerent motives of potential arms recipients, their history of respecting international arms-control initiatives and international law, degree and kind of human-rights violations, proximity to and potential role in dangerous regional conflicts, and the proportion of military budget of a potential purchaser in comparison with the government's commitment to human services needs. As for the implications of this proposal for our country, Lora

Lumpe, director of the Arms Sales Monitoring Process for the Federation of American Scientists, states, "Such a code of conduct . . . would turn the oversight process upside down. Right now, the U.S. Congress has to vote to *disapprove* arms sales. We would like to see this changed to where Congress would have to vote to *approve* every sale."[18]

I will end by bringing us back to a religious view. A simple definition of "militarism" as the tendency to approach problems in military terms, rather than diplomatic, may be helpful to understanding the following statement. In a December 1993 World Council of Churches paper sent to the heads of all member churches, the Commission of the Churches on International Affairs said,

> We are called to oppose all death-dealing and dehumanizing forces through our commitment to a theology of life. Conversion towards the demilitarization of international relations, away from militarism and national security doctrines and systems, and into a culture of non-violence as a force for change and liberation is more than a technical process of economic transformation. It involves fundamental redirection of individual lives, opposition to militarism, a new relationship between North and South, dismantling of military production facilities and bases, and the creation of new opportunities for those who are trapped either—and most directly—as victims of militarization in countries receiving arms or—more indirectly—as producers with little chance of alternative employment in arms selling countries.

Continuing the religion-based case for a changed order of priorities at both the individual and social levels, the World Council statement concludes,

> Metanoia means conversion and redirection of life. It is the antithesis of the oppression and fear which is so manifestly the result of the huge scale of military spending and arms transfers. The Seoul Covenant (1990) looks forward to "the dismantling of military industrial complexes" and "the stopping of the trade and transfer of arms." These are two of the necessary steps towards the "creation of an international economic and social order that will enable all nations and people to live in dignity and without fear." Nothing less than "overcoming the institution of war as a means to resolve conflicts" is necessary. Metanoia is conver-

sion—a turning away from the forces of death to the promise of
abundant life (John 10:10).[19]

The biblical injunction to choose life has simple and direct application to arms profiteering and its attendant immiseration of people
and the entire creation. *Ľchaim!* To life!

DISCUSSION QUESTIONS

1. Why are women and children predictably the victims of
   arms sales?
2. What is the Christian case for concern about arms transfers?
3. Does the capacity to pay for advanced arms mean that a given
   government has the right to make the purchase? Is the U.S.
   obliged to sell?
4. What is the argument in support of (or against) the claim that
   "if we didn't sell arms, others would, so we should"?
5. What is the intrinsic purpose of a weapon?
6. Why does our government routinely license foreign arms, or
   arms technology, sales?
7. Do arms sales predispose the globe to war or peace?
8. Is conversion possible from a Cold War to a civilian economy?

A LEGACY OF
MANIFEST DESTINY

"Manifest Destiny," defined as the belief that this country has been chosen by God to rule the earth, accomplished its greatest evils in the nineteenth century. The idea appears to have been as popular among nineteenth-century American people as it was among nineteenth-century American political leaders. Its legacy provides the historical context within which to attempt an understanding of certain countries in the Caribbean, Central America, and the Philippines, which were visited by members of the Commission on Peace with Justice in the spring and summer of 1993. The origins of Manifest Destiny thinking in the U.S., and some of its major implications for countries we visited, follow.

The distinction of having given a name to the phenomenon is usually assigned to John L. Sullivan, a New York lawyer, who owned, edited, and sometimes wrote most of *The United States Magazine and Democratic Review.* In the July 1845 issue of his journal, Sullivan prophesied "the fulfillment of our manifest destiny to overspread the continent allotted by providence for the free development of our yearly multiplying millions." Later in the same year, he was to invoke the doctrine to support the annexation of Texas, the acquisition of Oregon, and the prosecution of the war with Mexico.

The concept did not spring fully formed from a vacuum. Historians of ideas generally claim its first building block to be the invention of the progress idea during the period of the so-called Enlightenment, roughly between the late fifteenth and late eighteenth centuries. The growth of scientific knowledge, along with new inventions and a proliferation of explorations, had reached that stage at which it seemed reasonable to regard inevitable progress almost as an aspect of divine presence.

In the midst of such optimism, prototypical millenarians believed that the end of so much upwardness must inevitably be the Kingdom of God. In the seventeenth century, Jonathan Edwards, for example, thought he had found sound evidence for the approaching millennium in the "discovery" and settlement of the New World. He predicted confidently that Christ's Kingdom would finally be established in the New World in the last years of the twentieth century.

The Mayflower Covenants, and diaries and letters of Pilgrims in Massachusetts, were marked by the people's sense that they had been blessed with freedom and ordained by God to create a model society in the wilderness. Only a relatively few years were needed for America's leaders to adapt this optimism to the realm of politics. Thomas Jefferson, for instance, was to speak frequently of America's "right" to become a continental empire.

In 1840 a presbyterian minister from America, Samuel H. Cox, confided to an English audience that "the state of society [in America] is without parallel in universal history. I really believe that God has got America in anchorage and that upon that area he intends to display his prodigies for the millennium."

For better or worse, throughout much of the nineteenth century, belief in the millennium and confidence in its occurrence in America fed the fires of exploding nationalism. This period saw the expansion of the American republic all the way to the West Coast and beyond. In the minds of many, "Manifest Destiny" warranted the annexation of Texas, Oregon, New Mexico, and California, and intervention, and in some cases annexation, of Alaska, Cuba, the Philippines, and Hawaii.

MEXICO

In 1830 the president of Mexico, without much warning, closed the borders of his country and imposed on its population restrictions which violated the Mexican constitution.

Six years later, when the unhappy people of "Texas" declared themselves an independent republic, President Santa Anna led parts of his army to crush the incipient rebellion. Though he enjoyed a quick and easy success at the Alamo, he was soon to be defeated and captured (and in short turn freed).

Mexico made no further effort to regain the lost territory but refused to recognize its independence. Reacting to the battle cry of Manifest Destiny, a substantial number of Americans insisted that it was not enough to bring Texas into the union, but the whole of Mexico must be annexed as well. The boundaries of the United States, only recently enlarged by the acquisition of Florida and the Spanish colonies as far west as the Mississippi, should be expanded even further, they said. President Jackson announced that annexation was desirable because this would enlarge the area of free institutions in the world.

In the end, talk of a new American state of Mexico moderated, if it did not totally disappear. It became clear that such a development would mean a new "Southern," i.e., slave, state on the one hand; many who would not have objected to such an eventuality feared, on the other hand, a whole new state with an alien racial and religious (i.e., Catholic) culture. Thus in 1845 the U.S. administration announced that it was annexing only the territory of Texas. Though settlers from this area had never lived below the Nueces River, we claimed the new state's southern boundary to be the Rio Bravo del Norte. Predictably, Mexican President Santa Anna immediately denounced the claim and broke off diplomatic relations with the United States.

In his inaugural address President Polk said,

> I regard the question of the annexation [of Texas] as belonging exclusively to the United States and Texas. They are independent powers competent to contract, and foreign nations have no right to interfere with them or to take exception to their reunion. Foreign powers do not seem to appreciate the true character of our government. Our Union is a confederation of independent states whose policy is peace with each other and all the world. To enlarge its limits is to extend the dominion of peace over additional territories and increasing millions . . . Foreign powers should look on the annexation of Texas to the United States as diminishing the chances of war and opening to them new, ever increasing markets for their products.

Some Americans feared that adding Texas to the Union would be too great an expansion for it to be governed well. Polk said, however, that experience had shown that "[such] fears [are not] well founded . . . already the titles of various Indian tribes to vast tracts of country have been extinguished; new states have been admitted to the

Union, new territories have been created and our jurisdiction and laws have been extended over them . . . it is confidently believed that our system may be safely extended to the utmost boundaries of our territorial limits." The new president promised that once the Mexican problem had been taken care of, he would do his duty "to assert and maintain by all constitutional means the right of the United States to that portion of our territory which lies beyond the Rocky Mountains." He added, "Our title to the Country of the Oregon is clear and unquestionable."

When Polk sought an agreement with Mexico placing the border of Texas at the Rio Grande and permitting the United States to purchase California, Mexico refused summarily to discuss either matter. Polk then ordered American troops to occupy the territory of Texas between the disputed rivers. A clash between American and Mexican troops in April 1846 gave the U.S. president the war cry he needed: "American blood has been shed on American soil by foreign troops." This led Congressman Abraham Lincoln to ask the president to say "precisely where this outrage had occurred," which Polk never did answer. In his haste he declared war on Mexico.

With little difficulty, American troops captured what is now the state of New Mexico and California. American forces subsequently launched successful attacks on Cerro Gordo and Mexico City. In the last days of the war, Americans debated how much of Mexico might properly be demanded as "our due." Predictably, opposing positions went from "none at all" to "the whole country," according to warriors on the side of Manifest Destiny.

In the end, with Mexico City and Cerro Gordo in America's hands, peace negotiators from both sides met at Guadalupe Hidalgo to negotiate a treaty giving the United States all territories north of an irregular line of the Rio Grande and the Rio Gila to the Pacific. In return, the United States paid Mexico $15 million for the other territories we had captured and assumed responsibility for settling some $3 million in claims of American citizens against Mexico. The affair seemed to demonstrate the validity of Manifest Destiny thinking and its associated psychology of entitlement.

OUR WAR WITH SPAIN

It is arguable that our brief war with Spain invoked the worst aspects of Manifest Destiny. Our relations with Cuba, which led ultimately to the Spanish-American War, betray a mixture of humanitarian concern and a bellicose grasping for power and wealth. They also demonstrate remarkable presumption.

The island of Cuba, ninety miles off the southernmost tip of the United States at Key West, was "discovered" in 1492 during Columbus's first voyage. Claimed by him for Spain, it became subject to frequent raids by England, France, and Holland (who saw it as a key to trade and traffic in the West Indies). None succeeded in detaching it from the Spanish vine. By the end of the eighteenth century, Cuba and the United States had begun trading with each other.

From the beginning, Spain managed its affairs with Cuba in its own interests. For a long period the island was forbidden to trade with any foreign power without specific permission from the mother country. Faced with a serious labor shortage in the sixteenth century, Spain began importing slaves from Africa into its Caribbean colony.

Isolated later from its colonies by wars in Europe, Spain sent a series of fairly liberal governors to Havana during the late 1700s. By 1809, the island was engaging in free trade with other countries, and in 1810 Cuba was allowed to send delegates with limited powers to the Cortes. By 1818, Spain legalized the unofficial free trade that had sprung up. Whether because of, or despite, the relaxed rule of Spain, the islands are generally described by historians as restive and discontented during the early nineteenth century. Many began to talk more or less openly about freedom, autonomy within the Spanish empire, or annexation by the United States.

During this time, certain Americans welcomed the idea of annexing the islands. Presidents Pierce and Polk each tried unsuccessfully to purchase them; sentiment in the United States cooled, however, in light of the vexing problem of whether the territory would be slave or free.

Meanwhile, Spanish policies again became seriously restrictive and Cuban tempers flared. The seeds of Cuban independence movements were planted. By 1855, skirmishes had occurred between Cuban and Spanish forces.

Finally, in 1868 war broke out between them. This was to become the longest war fought in the Americas. More than 200,000 Spanish and Cuban soldiers were to die in the ten years before its end. There was some agitation for annexation among some Americans, but it appears that the memory of the Civil War was too recent for the kind of energy needed to fight.

A conciliatory peace was achieved in 1878, though this proved to be short lived. Spain promised sweeping reforms in its policies toward Cuba, amnesty to political prisoners, liberty for rebels, and the abolition of slavery. Cuba, however, was forced to pay the cost of the war. In short order the promised reforms became memory. Spanish behavior once again became despotic and independence movements became active and voluble. The situation worsened immeasurably when, in the midst of a severe financial crisis, the American government withdrew sugar tariff schedules that had favored Cuba, and unemployment and economic hardship became widespread. This further encouraged Cuban discontent with Spain.

In 1898, when Spain suspended all constitutional guarantees applied to the people of Cuba, the heroes of the ten-year war remobilized. José Marti's Cuban Revolutionary Movement, founded in the United States in 1892, unified the island's nationalistic elements long enough for a constitution to be drawn up and a council of national leaders appointed. The revolutionary struggle that ensued was bitter and cruel, as Cubans set out to make their homeland useless to the occupiers by making it uninhabitable. Spain reacted with harsher policies, until a newly appointed premier recalled the worst of the country's governors, ordered significant changes in policy, and promised the island autonomy, but without independence. This proved unacceptable to most Cubans.

Violence increased. In the United States, on February 20, 1896, United States Senator Henry Cabot Lodge, who believed that the Anglo-Saxon race possessed unique qualities that destined it for greatness, was pushing the notion of Manifest Destiny. He argued that if Spain did not accept an American offer to mediate the dispute in Cuba, we should take forceful action immediately, because ". . . our immediate interests in the Island are very great," and "the islands, along with our investments in them," were being destroyed. Freeing Cuba, he said, "would mean a great market for the United States, an opportunity for American capital to be invited there by significant exemptions." It would also help bring about an opportunity for the development of "that splendid island." "Do not forget," he said, that "Cuba has a population of 1,500,000 and is one of the richest spots on the face of the earth." The island's position across the Gulf of Mexico, he said, "in our hands, or in friendly hands [among its own people] attached to us by ties of interest and gratitude, is a bulwark to the commerce, to the safety, and to the peace of the United States." Manifest Destiny psychology did not begin with a sincere regard for the Cubans themselves.

The retiring president, Grover Cleveland, warned Spain that the United States could not be expected to wait too long for it to bring about an end of the war "either alone and in her own way or with our friendly cooperation." A time may come, said President Cleveland, when "our obligations to the sovereignty of Spain will be superseded by higher obligations, which we can hardly hesitate to recognize and discharge." At that time, "a correct policy, and care for our interests, as well as a regard for the interests of other nations and their citizens, joined by considerations of humanity and a desire to see a rich and fertile country intimately related to the United States saved from complete devastation, will constrain our government to such action as will subserve the interests thus involved and at the same time promise to Cuba and its inhabitants an opportunity to enjoy the blessings of peace."

Only months after this, William McKinley was to deliver his first message on Cuba in the early days of 1897. McKinley set forth three alternative actions open to the United States: (1) we could recognize the insurgents as belligerents, (2) we could recognize the independence of the nation of Cuba, and (3) we could intervene to end the rebellion, either as a neutral to end the war by imposing a rational compromise, or in favor of one side or the other. "I speak not of forcible annexation," he said, "for that cannot be thought of . . . that, by our code of morality, would be criminal aggression."

His solution?

> Sure of the right, keeping free from all offense ourselves, actuated only by upright and patriotic considerations, neither by passion nor selfishness, this government will continue its watch over the rights and properties of American citizens and will abate none of its efforts to bring about by peaceful agencies a peace which shall be honorable and enduring, [but] if it shall hereafter appear to be a duty imposed by our obligations to ourselves, to civilization, to humanity to intervene with force, it shall be without fault on our part and only because the necessity for such action will be so clear as to command the support and approval of the civilized world.

Against such a summation, the nation was rife with talk of war. Theodore Roosevelt had written to Admiral Mahan that if he could have his way he would occupy Cuba tomorrow. The press was laying the groundwork for an attack on Spain through Cuba. Joseph Pulitzer, owner of *The New York World,* said of a possible war with Spain that he "rather liked the idea of a war—not a big one, but one that would arouse interest" and give him "a chance to gauge the reflex on circulation figures."

In the end, McKinley's address was of little positive help, and the situation in Cuba worsened. On February 15, 1898, the American battleship *Maine* was blown up in Havana harbor. American newspapers predictably stepped up their campaigns for war, and though a naval court of inquiry determined that the *Maine* had been destroyed by a submarine bomb, it could not say who was responsible. The press, however, left no doubt that only Spain could have been responsible. The U.S. declared war.

In the end, the war against Spain lasted only a few months. In his instructions to his ministers who were to negotiate the terms of peace at a conference in Europe, McKinley pointed out that Spain had already agreed to relinquish all of its claims to sovereignty over Cuba, to cede to the United States Puerto Rico and other islands ruled by it in the West Indies, to cede to the United States one island in the Ladrones to be selected by the United States at a later date, and to evacuate Cuba, Puerto Rico, and other Spanish islands in the West Indies immediately. It was agreed that the United States would immediately occupy the city, bay, and harbor of Manila pending the closing of a treaty of peace that would determine the control, disposition, and government of the Philippines.

THE PHILIPPINES

The matter of the Philippines, McKinley said, was different from the Spanish islands in the Western Hemisphere. The presence and the success of our arms in Manila imposed upon us obligations we could not ignore. We cannot be indifferent either, said the president, to the commercial opportunities in the Philippines. On the other hand, he continued, the United States did not need large territories in the Philippines; indeed, only an adequate base and broad and equal privileges were needed. From these requirements, McKinley specified that we "cannot accept less than the cession in full right and sovereignty of the island of Luzon . . . the right of entry for vessels and merchandise belonging to citizens of our country into such parts of the Philippines as are not ceded to us on terms of equal favor of Spanish ships and merchandise in these islands."

Cuba in the end had not been annexed to the United States; it became instead a virtual protectorate of its larger neighbor. The Platt Amendment, which we had forced into the Cuban sections of the peace treaty with Spain, and which would later be inserted, at our insistence, into the constitution of the Republic of Cuba, gave us the right to intervene to maintain Cuban independence and to sanction all Cuban trade concessions to foreign powers. This right was invoked on several occasions before the treaty of 1903 was abrogated in 1934.

All of Puerto Rico and all of the Philippine archipelago, on the other hand, became U.S. territories. In Puerto Rico, there was little opposition to the new status. In the Philippines, however, though McKinley had called taking over the islands an act of "benevolent assimilation," it soon became clear that anything like self-government was out of the question. The island's most important military hero, Aguinaldo, rallied the people in an insurrection that resulted in the deaths of some million Filipinos before it was quelled. Mark Twain, pointing to the carnage in the Philippines, asked in an article, "Shall we go on conferring our civilization upon the peoples that sit in darkness, or shall we give these poor things a rest?" This land at long last received its independence on July 4, 1946.

By this war's end, our sense of U.S. Manifest Destiny had brought 7.5 million Filipinos and some 1 million Puerto Ricans under American rule. Though it didn't make the Pacific an American lake, we frequently acted as if it had.

A careful reading of the many speeches and newspaper accounts of U.S. assumptions, presumptions, motives, and the like during this period reminds one of how far we have come. We don't talk so openly these days in racist or messianic terms. Although in one sense it is unfair to criticize people in former times for failures that are more evident today—I think again of racism and nationalistic arrogance—it nevertheless seems likely that racially oppressed "lesser breeds without the law" could have described the problem, if others had been inclined to listen.

We decided to visit some countries that had in common an experience of U.S. Manifest Destiny presumptions. In light of the experiences of our commission, in preparing to visit, and then traveling to Cuba, the Philippines, and other countries affected by U.S. overseeing, it seems fair to say that certain assumptions underlying Manifest Destiny thinking are still operative among some of our business and governmental figures. These include that the U.S. is entitled to involve itself in the affairs of certain other countries when it wants to, that the fate of the people in them is not as important as the fate of the important people in our own country, and that white people are inherently more valuable than people of darker skin color. There can hardly be any other way to interpret continuing U.S. attitudes and behaviors regarding these countries.

We believe that the present state of affairs in the countries we visited is the direct result of processes set in motion at century's beginning.

LUZON TODAY

Charles Henry Brent, appointed missionary bishop of the Philippines in 1901 by the U.S. Episcopal Church, got himself into the mountains of northern Luzon, where he declined three subsequent bishop elections in order to continue establishing congregations in the beautiful, rugged cordillera. Perhaps it was here where Brent wrote the well-known collect that begins, "Lord Jesus Christ, you stretched out your arms on the hard wood of the cross that everyone might come within the reach of your saving embrace. . . ." Nearly a century later, a few of us—members of the Standing Commission on Peace with Justice—visited those congregations and their present bishop, Robert Longid. There we discovered a vital ministry of service amid terrible poverty, armed struggle, kidnap, ambush, intimidation, and extrajudicial killing.

At the turn of the century the Philippines had been wrested from three centuries of Spanish domination by U.S. military might. For $20 million, and with more than 11,000 U.S. troops in the archipelago, Spain pulled out, signing the Treaty of Paris on December 10, 1898. Shortly thereafter, U.S. President McKinley admitted, "When I realized that the Philippines had dropped into our laps I confess I did not know what to do with them." But he soon figured it out:

"There was nothing left for us to do but take them all, and to educate the Filipinos, and uplift and civilize and Christianize them, and by God's grace do the very best we could by them, as our fellow men for whom Christ died."[1]

Not surprisingly, the natives were dubious and the fight was on. By 1901 Theodore Roosevelt had 120,000 soldiers there shooting up the place. One estimate is that about one-sixth of the population were killed; the *Philadelphia Ledger* reported at the time, "Our men have been relentless; they have killed to exterminate men, women, children, prisoners and captives, active insurgents and suspected people, from lads of 10 and up, an idea prevailing that the Filipino, as such, was little better than a dog, a noisome reptile in some instances, whose best disposition was the rubbish heap."[2] (I will spare you contemporary accounts of torture.)

The history of U.S. relations with the Philippines since the end of World War II is characterized initially by anticommunist hysteria practiced with treachery and violence against the Huks. These had bravely fought against the Japanese occupiers and genuinely had welcomed the liberating forces of MacArthur. The U.S. then reinstalled indigenous leaders who had collaborated with the Japanese. The picture includes Air Force Lieutenant Colonel Edward Geary Lansdale, who in 1950 became the chief advisor to the Filipinos on the nasty business of counterinsurgency, and not incidentally was the person widely believed to be the model for Burdick and Lederer's novel *The Ugly American*. In general, "the introduction of ideology as a motive for counterinsurgency organization, notably the negative ideology of anticommunism, would become a very real factor in the paramilitary structures of the Philippines in the 1970s, eventually to dominate the scene even in the 1990s."[3] About the paramilitary we were to learn more in the mountains.

■   ■   ■

In April 1993 our group met in Honolulu with Filipino expatriate clergy and with the consul general of the Philippines. Most of the priests were originally from the Mountain Province, where the leftist insurgency is presumably centered; this is where we were headed. The issues, we were told, included the recent closure of the two major U.S. bases in the Philippines, the economic and political implications of this, the large numbers of Amerasian children (fathered by U.S. military personnel), land reform, the vexing problem of electrical blackouts (for which President Fidel Ramos has recently received emergency powers), the tremendous diversity of the Filipino people (which makes national unity so difficult), the shocking disparities in income, and the "total war" policy of the government against the leftists—the National Democratic Front (NDF) and its military arm, the New People's Army (NPA).

President Ramos—Cory Aquino's defense minister, and before that, a lieutenant general during the Marcos period—has apparently extended the olive branch to the leftists, which he needs to do because he was elected with only a 23 percent plurality (he needs all the friends he can get). Or he is only feigning an openness to the left in order to gain time to build his military (the military budget is now higher than it has ever been). The problem for the Episcopal Church—which we were to verify later for ourselves—is to minister among the people who are caught, as the church is caught, between the government forces (army, paramilitary, and national police) and the NPA. Agents from both sides infiltrate religious services to see what is being said and by whom. One priest said his family were terrorized by the NPA, but that some of his friends had joined them "because they were treated better; they had food." Another priest said, "Where the military is in control of an area there are reports of abuses against women." Still another said, "People think the NPA is more concerned with justice than the government is."

The consul general of the Philippines is an impressive woman. She told us, "The people of our country keep a very close eye upon the U.S., but we don't get the feeling that your country knows we are here. President Clinton has not said a word about us since he took office."

■ ■ ■

Manila was hot, muggy, and as smoggy as Mexico City. The poverty was appalling. A sign near the entrance to our hotel compound advised people to check their guns with the guards. In the lobby was a book prominently displayed at the registration counter: "I Wanna Be In America: 1993 U.S. Immigration Laws Explained." I walked around a three-block area outside. Uniformed guards holding automatic rifles stood in stores and doorways to deter would-be robbers, and I was not reassured by learning that the primary kidnappers of foreign tourists are the national police.

We traveled to the headquarters of the Episcopal Church in the Philippines to meet with staff. What a youthful group they are. One, Danny Ocampo, the economic development officer, had served a year as a political detainee. On the bulletin board was a letter from the prime bishop to the people of his church decrying the kidnapping of foreign tourists, with the associated extortion.[4]

A crucial first step for peace for the ordinary people—for a chance to live free from fear, threats, violence, and one day perhaps even from crushing poverty—we were told, is President Ramos's National Unification Commission, which presumably wants to work out differences. The Episcopal Church supports the NUC, since "First, there is a Christian mandate to be peacemakers; second, not all avenues have been explored; third, they should be; fourth, therefore we call the parties to meet at the negotiating table; fifth, our church is open to joining with any and all others in working for peace."

There is concern in this office about the roundup of political prisoners, the antisubversion law, the foreign debt, the fact that only a tiny minority control all the land, and a justice-based (rather than force-based) peace. The principal tactical concern is to try to avoid a perhaps lethal alignment with either the government or the NPA, in fact or in appearance, while ministering among people caught in a sticky web of helplessness and intimidation, without hope of control over their political or economic future.

On current U.S.-Philippines relations: "Since the closing of the U.S. bases here there has been a lessening of tensions. Also, since Clinton the U.S. embassy has been less strident, so the opposition is quieter too. Our $30 billion foreign debt—owed mainly to the U.S. and Japan—and the U.S.-led World Bank and International Monetary Fund, are the sore spots now for anti-U.S. feeling. Our 1993 GNP is lower than it was last year and 40 percent of our national budget goes to service the debt. This makes development all but impossible." (An April 1992 Church policy statement says, "The greater bulk of the debt has not redounded to the benefit of our people [but] has only enriched the coffers of the few. . . . The saddest [thing is that] every one of us is now asked to pay for all these monetary obligations. Herein lies the immorality of the debt problem.")[5]

■   ■   ■

Next day we headed north toward the rugged mountains where both the Episcopal Church and the insurgency are centered. Driving through ash still left from Pinatubo, passing evidence of a 7.4 earthquake, and the long road to Cory Aquino's "Hacienda Luisita," we finally reached Baguio City and met the bishop of the North Central Diocese. This man is young, in his mid-thirties, and recently elected to succeed a bishop who had left to take a Filipino expatriate parish in the U.S. (This caused some resentment from some who felt abandoned in their struggle, in favor of the easier life abroad.) Much construction is taking place to rebuild from the devastating earthquake of a few years ago. Offices are needed for the crucial staff positions of economic development and social concerns officers, and for the diocesan horticulturist, who will help the people with their farming.

We were told that in this land of extraordinary deprivation, 99 percent of the national congress are millionaires: large landowners, miners, industrialists; these are not likely to push the justice-based peace agenda. This highland city itself displays the economic and political state of the nation; in one sector is the shopping area patronized by the Manila upper crust on holiday, and beyond is squalor.

The day after that, we reached Bontoc, the headquarters of the Episcopal Diocese of the Northern Philippines, and its bishop, Robert Longid. This diocese is the largest in the country in land area, but there is no airstrip in it; there are no phones, though the bishop has a shortwave radio. To get back down to Baguio you must navigate a treacherous, mostly single lane, largely unpaved mountain road for at least six hours; the scenery is as spectacular as the route is terrifying. The mountains are jagged, clad in lush green foliage; across the steep valleys, cut into the slopes of the cordillera, are the endless rice terraces. Occasionally you see people working them, women, children, and men in loin cloths in this former headhunter territory. After lunch we drove up another road still higher, to Sagada.

Here we learned some important facts: in this area, by government decree all lands on a slope greater than 18 degrees belong to the government (I had not seen land that flat in two days; the whole region belongs to the folks in Manila); in Aguid, a nearby village, the local Episcopal church was "desecrated" when the army used it as a garrison; there is heavy military presence locally, and heavy paramilitary and NPA activity as well. The paramilitary are set up by the army to control the local situation; this frees the army to move on in accordance with a "special operations" counterinsurgency philosophy learned from U.S. advisors. There are over 150,000 paramilitary personnel now operating in the country. (The NPA "sparrows"—a hit squad—killed a U.S. army colonel a few years earlier near the Manila hotel where we stayed, expressly because of U.S. "low-intensity-conflict" training of the military.)

Sagada had once tried to be a violence-free zone, with military, paramilitary, and NPAs staying out. Then the army, we were told, staged a mock battle, presumably against encroaching NPAs; the army moved back in. There are now raids by both sides on encampments, roadside ambushes, assassinations, arrests and detentions, sabotage, disappearances, homes being raided, and the like. The people seem tired, patient, nervous, hopeful, and fatalistic all at once, and you wonder, how do they carry on? A young priest, known for his forthright advocacy of the people, has for this reason earned the enmity of the army. He sat at our table, but he said very little; instead his attention seemed to be upon his church in the distance, or upon the trees beyond, or upon the little houses near it. What was he thinking? What did he think about these strange Americans who had come to do . . . what? Show support? Convey sympathy? Understanding? Try to help (but what could these Americans, or any of them, do?)?

The army recently objected to the local hospital treating people regardless of political affiliation. Accusing the two doctors there of aiding the NPAs, the government has blocked medical shipments. When clergy are suspected of "antigovernment activities," the army spreads rumors about their being Communist, and advertisements are created showing priests in cassocks with bandoleers of ammunition and automatic rifles in their hands.

A visit to the regional military headquarters in Bontoc the next day helped us understand the church's predicament. The commanding officer, Colonel Lardizibal, an Episcopalian, spoke repeatedly of the church's "antigovernment activities." Finally I asked what these were, exactly. "Criticizing the government. Influencing people to join leftist organizations." The army believes that both church and community-service agencies are pro-leftist if they are in only minor disagreement with the government. "If the clergy would cooperate, about 30 percent of the [insurgency] problem would be solved," said the colonel; "Episcopal Church means antigovernment to some of the people." He detailed the good things the army does for the people, including building schools, fixing highways, repairing bridges, and the like. "But the violence by the NPAs must cease. Near here they buried one man alive and shot another; a soldier was hacked to death. But when a policeman was killed, the people ran the NPAs off." An enlisted man took several photos of us during our interview.

Returning to the diocesan office, we met with two staff from the Task Force [for political] Detainees, a nongovernmental organization established by the Roman Catholic Church in 1974, two years after the declaration of martial law. This group is charged with investigating and documenting political arrest and detention, extrajudicial killings (known as "salvagings"), and disappearances. Present also were staff from the Cordillera People's Alliance, Human Rights Desk, Mountain Province, and from the Development Association for Tribes in the Cordillera. We were struck by their youth (all were in their twenties) and their gentle manner. Present also was a local Episcopal priest; he and one of the women were with twenty-five-year-old Christopher Batan (of Task Force Detainees) the previous month when the group was ambushed by some paramilitary in the area. Christopher had been killed. On my left sat Christopher's brother. We were given a copy of the church's file on this incident, and I quote from an affidavit filed by the young woman:

> I . . . depose and say . . . that about two o'clock this afternoon [we three] dispatched for Barangay Betwagan . . . to interview some families who were victims of past human-rights violations which remain unacted [upon] to the present . . . that about three o'clock . . . while [we] were resting . . . one AGUSTIN AGPAWAN . . . and two companions passed by us. . . . That all of a sudden, this AGUSTIN AGPAWAN who was beside a rock on the other side of the river . . . opened fire with his rifle and the shot rang out hitting our companion CHRISTOPHER BATAN who wriggled to the ground moaning in great pain. . . . That while I may have been very terrified, I have to hold my ground and helped attend to our companion . . . and in the process, one of the companions of Agustin Agpawan approached us and there and then shot at close range our companion . . . after which they . . . left, running toward Betwagan; that I hereby state, that I can identify the person who put the final shot to our deceased companion if presented. . . .

We were told that the military were protecting the killers, and we were given a copy of a military paper, printed a month before the ambush, identifying the staff of Christopher Batan's agency as Communist sympathizers—an accusation, we could see, equivalent to a death sentence.[6]

The Reverend Victor Ananayo, social concerns officer of the local diocese, described the church's ministry. It is to serve among the people without becoming aligned with any group, government or insurgent. This is difficult when the military holds the view that whoever is not totally for us is against us. For instance, when the diocese interceded to have soldiers captured by the NPA turned over to the bishop, and the soldiers were once delivered, the church was caught between the families of these men, who wanted them to come home, and the army, who wanted them also. When the army arrived at the diocesan office they were blocked by the women of the soldiers' families who took their men home. The military were furious and accused the diocese of being antigovernment. (Women, incidentally, are quite effective in opposing the army. When government bulldozers were poised to strip mine for copper, the women stripped and lay down in front of the vehicles; the drivers ran away.)

Later in the bishop's office, Robert Longid spoke of the year Marcos resigned: "We found out in 1986 that driving out a tyrant does not end tyranny." When asked about danger to him personally, this impressive bishop said, "I told a missionary conference in Sewanee that one of these days Bob Longid may be killed, and the bullet will have come from you"—referring both to U.S. arms transfers to his nation, and to the 1983 military statement naming him a "confirmed Communist terrorist."

"The church has been critical of much government activity," said Bishop Longid,

> especially regarding human rights. We protested, with the people, an enormous dam project that would have placed this entire city under water, displacing all the people. This whole region has been drained of its natural resources to benefit the wealthy. The Mountain Province is the headwaters for ten big rivers that water the lowlands; they have taken our gold and copper deposits. All these resources have been extracted, and nothing is put back into this region. In this office we settle tribal differences. . . . You see we have staff workers for social concerns and for economic development. The church must help the people, but for this we are accused of being NPA.

■　■　■

We met back in Manila with Dr. Maria Serena Diokno, a professor at the University of the Philippines and a prominent peace negotiator between the government and the NDF. She decried the violence on all sides and spoke of the worsening economy, and the overall peace process. She gave us clear statistical information, and I became depressed.

More factual information comes from a late 1992 Amnesty International publication: "Since 1988 at least 550 people, all of them unarmed, have been killed by government or government-backed forces in the Philippines. It is likely that many more have died. . . . The armed opposition has also been responsible for political killings. The victims have included residents of rural communities, trade unionists, government officials and opposition group members suspected of spying for the military."[7]

The day before we left for home, a Spanish priest was kidnapped in the south and held for 6 million pesos. If he is not ransomed in fifteen days his throat will be cut.

At 4:30 A.M. we left for the airport. It was dark in Manila and the headlights of our vehicle illumined the mudflap of a Jeepney in front of us. On it were the words, "God save us."

We had been asked to request help from the U.S. government in human rights, in debt reduction or restructuring, in ending arms transfers, in land reform, in ending official corruption, in ending the government's "total war" policy, in support of environmental protection, in the things that make for justice and peace.

The ministry of the Episcopal Church there is simple in concept: give hope to the people, *practically*, by helping them in agriculture and development, and by witnessing in courageous patience to a divine promise of faithfulness to those who walk in darkness and in the shadow of death. But embodying the concept is not easy in a context of insinuation and violence. It requires a plucky nerve, tenacity, singleness and purity of heart, and no little portion of God's gracious mercy and protection.

The Episcopal Church in the Philippines is in real danger of being crucified. You try to come to terms with your horror at this prospect, as you are captured by the church's determination to be faithful in service to the people. Since Bishop Brent, our identity as Episcopalians has been tied to theirs. It would be extremely meaningful if all of us spared a thought, said some prayers, and wrote strong letters for the Philippines.

PANAMA, THE DOMINICAN REPUBLIC, CUBA, NICARAGUA

The four countries, two in Central America, two in the Caribbean, visited by six members of the Standing Commission in June 1993 have histories and current political concerns that are closely intertwined with the United States. In Episcopal Church polity, three of these countries, Panama, Nicaragua, and the Dominican Republic, are presently dioceses in Province IX of the Episcopal Church, U.S.A. The Diocese of Haiti is part of Province II, and the Diocese of Cuba is Extra Provincial to Metropolitan Council, which consists of the primate of Canada, the archbishop of the West Indies and the president of the U.S. Church's Province IX. The legacy of Manifest Destiny in the Western Hemisphere, coupled with the end of the Cold War and rising ethnic tensions, has severely affected these nations to our south. Building and rebuilding democratic structures during this period of economic deprivation is causing much dislocation in all these societies.

Though U.S. citizens often stereotype these and other Central American countries on the basis of their Spanish language and Spanish cultural heritage, each of these nations has a unique history and culture. However, there are some common themes that run through their current struggles—not least of these being the long history of U.S. involvement and intervention in their internal affairs. The role of the Episcopal Church, originally chaplaincies of British and American business, is also unique in each. While small, the church is growing. It provides a middle road between the Roman Catholic Church, whose hierarchy often sided with the oligarchy, and continues to do so, and the rising evangelical sects that draw many with their message of personal salvation.

Central Americans, particularly, believe that North Americans view them as one people without regard for the distinctions among them. While this report will look at the commonalities of issues, it also recognizes that each nation approaches them differently and is truly an individual unit.

The commission identified several discrete concerns: land reform, racism in its several forms, the abrogation of human rights, drugs, national pride and self-esteem, and environmental issues. Each nation is seeking a representative form of government that will provide economic opportunity for the populace as a whole, but the role of the military remains problematic.

Panama: An Eyewitness Report

On May 30, 1993, several members of our Peace Commission were met at the Panama City airport by a member of Bishop James Ottley's staff and driven to the diocesan guest house. One of the many sites along the way was an old railroad station. When one in our group asked about why the trains were not in operation, he was told that Japan would like to design trains for Panama but that the treaties that exist today prohibit such negotiations. By 1999 Panama will be free to pursue such possibilities.

A bus strike was in effect during our entire stay in Panama. The country's bus system is loosely akin to New York City's taxi and limousine service in that some buses belong to a licensed group, others to a fleet, and still others are individually owned. The strike not only tied up the city but also closed schools and streets. The potential for violence was real. The Panamanian government wanted to deregulate buses, but others complained that such deregulation could well create a monopoly, freezing out small companies.

We also learned that Panama's former attorney general had been removed from office and that the new attorney general was under investigation. This was the atmosphere in which we arrived.

From 1903 to 1968 Panama's government could best be described as an oligarchy made up of people trained from birth to rule. In 1968 the government was comprised of military personnel, with a rather controlled economy. Drugs were not then trafficked into Panama, although drug money was laundered there; this kept money flowing into the country. Some Panamanians said openly that they are convinced the present sale of drugs in Central America is helping the U.S. offset its national debt.

Although the U.S. government has charged that many of the conditions which exist today are the same that existed under Noriega, a number of Panamanians told us that they do not prefer Noriega but they know that the situation in their country has worsened since he was captured. In fact, members of the Coordinadora Popular De Derechos Humanos De Panama, a human-rights organization, said the situation is out of control and that present conditions have created greater human-rights violations than before; of particular concern were 60 percent of the children who now suffer from malnutrition. The weight of the national debt, we were told, is taking a heavy toll on the country.

Until 1968 Colón and Panama City were among the few places that had electricity. After that time most of the country was electrified. A middle-class professional group also arose around 1968, and black Panamanians began to assume more responsible positions.

On June 1 our group met with members of the Diocesan Human Rights Commission whose members discussed the role of the church since the U.S. invasion of Panama in 1989. Members said Panama has a concept of what it can do and desires the opportunity to act without fear of U.S. intervention. They feel that the U.S. is unnecessarily suspicious of communism and that it is this which forced the change in North America's good-neighbor policy toward Central America. They pointed out the destabilizing effect United States elections have on their country, bringing to our attention the fact that every time we elect a new president our foreign policy is subject to change.

Members of the Human Rights Commission said that the church must be the voice of the people but noted that their government is attempting to split the church and government. The government, on the other hand, is forming a bond with the Roman Catholic Church and attempting to exclude other denominations. The Anglican Church in Panama has four Episcopal schools (which are all bilingual), 5,000 communicants and twenty-three clergy (five of whom are women). The clergy total includes bishops. There are thirty-five congregations and Bishop Ottley had a goal of fifty congregations before his retirement. (When he became diocesan bishop, there were only twenty congregations and twelve clergy.)

We met with the indigenous Indians of Panama and were told that unemployment among them was at 11 percent in 1987, 27 percent in 1989 (prior to the U.S. invasion), and that after the invasion it went up from 35 to 40 percent. Many asked that members of the United Nations visit Panama to see the housing conditions under which thousands of Panamanians must live. We went into the some of the houses that would be opened for U.N. inspection and were appalled to find that buildings that were beautifully painted outside had no inner walls, no railings along the staircases, and had entire families living in a single room. There were virtually no toilets or kitchens, and cloth material was hung to separate one living area from another.

Outside of what the government claimed was a habitable apartment building, a painting done by a child dominated the area. It showed U.S. helicopters flying over Panama, dropping bombs that killed innocent children during an attempt to bring Manuel Noriega out of hiding.

The Indians of Panama presented a series of grievous situations regarding demarcation and guarantee of their original land. They said that the government of Panama has responded with repression, and that death was the result for one Pueblo Indian during a demonstration. The Human Rights group, COPODEHUPA, was said to be investigating the case.

Congreso Ngobe-Bugle said he was the only Indian at the press conference that followed the U.S. invasion of Panama. He asked that a high-level commission of the Panamanian government deal with the problems of Indian people, but he indicated that the government has not responded. In order to be heard, a national coordinator of indigenous people was chosen and the legislature was asked to act on the thirty-year-old laws establishing territory for Indian people. When there was no response to their petitions, the Indians went on strike.

Congreso Embera-Inaanan and Congreso Kuna work with Congreso Ngobe-Bugle to secure rights for indigenous people. They want the government to stop moving them from their land, but their land continues to be taken. They continue to be segregated because gold has been discovered on the land that was once assigned to them. The Indians maintain that not only is the land rightfully theirs, according to previous agreements, but that in its attempt to mine gold, the government is destroying the ecological balance.

On June 4 we met with the president of the Democratic party, who gave us a brief history of the country and said the present situation is a change from the former repressive dictatorship to a basic democratic system. He told us there are now eighteen political parties, some without ideological identity. Political institutions are still weak and no party has a built-in majority. The General Assembly, which is lively, intense, and far from firm, is still seen as weak and ineffective when it comes to producing laws.

The executive branch of government has been the same for the last thirty years, with the cumulative effect of almost no modernization of the state. Many still view the government in paternalistic terms, expecting to have all solutions come from it. The president said there is a need for serious revision of the present constitution

in order to make it a more participatory instrument for the people.
He cited the following failures of the present government:

- At the socioeconomic level, an attempt was made to recover
  growth in macro terms (an attempt of 45 percent in the first
  year), but there was an inability to resolve the unemployment
  problem. In this regard Panamanian people seeking jobs must
  have proper business attire, but since most do not, this negatively affects their basic "presentation of self." There is also a
  lack of money for transportation to interviews. The number of
  people now below the poverty line is 50 percent of the population, with $325 per month being the established minimum for
  a family.
- Before and during the last dictatorship there developed a middle class that produced wider polarization between the small
  wealthy upper class and the large poor lower class. Notably the
  major victims of the bus strike were those whose jobs were
  three to four hours of travel to and from home.
- Government corruption—the government permitted a resur-
  gence of corruption and influence-peddling; this made priva-
  tization questionable, as in the case of the bus strike. Nepotism
  has created an atmosphere of family ownership and is seen as
  now running rampant.

  When we asked for his vision for the 1994 election, the president said he hoped six or seven candidates would emerge from
  the eighteen parties and that he saw the following three basic
  options:
- A return to government of the style in effect prior to 1968.
- Living with nostalgia for former dictator Torrijos during his best
  moments, because at least then the dictatorship was enveloped
  in certain social values (but he admitted these values were eventually lost).
- Attempting to introduce basic change within the present democratic system, with decentralized decision-making.

We were told that when Noriega was in power the drugs only
went *through* Panama because there was a partnership between
those who controlled the drugs and the government. In the absence
of Noriega, however, drugs are now flowing *into* Panama and being

consumed there. Hotels, shopping centers, lending institutions all launder drug money. It is hidden everywhere, he said.

We spent time in Colón, a city of blacks made up, in part, by those brought over to work during the building of the Panama Canal. We met with members of MODESTO, the Movement of (the) Disemployed of Colón, which began in 1992 with nine people and has grown to a reported 7,000 members. MODESTO is made up of mostly poor laborers, while the organization of FRASCO (which supports the aims of MODESTO) is made up of educated, mostly employed professionals. Those with money in Colón are Latin, Jewish, Arab, and Chinese who work in the duty-free zone of Freeport.

Colón was "discovered" in 1853 by North Americans during the gold rush. Not long afterward shanties were built for the 60,000 West Indians previously brought over to help build the railroad but who later became part of management during the building of the canal. They now comprise most of the middle class of the city. Escaped slaves, who were taken to the Panamanian coast in the fourteenth or fifteenth century by the Spaniards, lived in the mountains outside the city for many years but have recently come down into the city seeking safety.

It seems that the reason a number of the West Indians left home for Panama was to work on the canal; this made it easier for them to obtain U.S. citizenship after the canal was completed because it was then a port of entry for the U.S.

Colón was originally an island but landfill between it and Panama City, one and a half hours away, connected it to the mainland. Pockets of poor people live along the city's water bank and subsist on the fish they are able to catch.

Before leaving, at the invitation of the Reverend Gail Keeney-Mulligan, I met with some young women in Colón who told me that the racism there, based on the *shade* of one's skin, has given them great trouble securing work. Potential employers use photographs to weed out darker-skinned applicants, and hire those they consider prettier (which the young women said means "of lighter complexion")—this even though the latter may not be as well qualified as the former.

The Episcopal Diocese of Panama has provided a voice of conscience for the Panamanian people. A recently formed Department of Human Rights monitors violations and advises the bishop. Diocesan representatives work closely with the unemployed and with indigenous people in Colón. Since there is little public confidence in Panama's political and judicial processes, the church is increasingly sought as a support and an ally of the people in the struggle for a better life.

The Dominican Republic

On June 4 we entered Santo Domingo in the Dominican Republic and spent time with Dr. Salsado, president of ministry to Haitians; the chancellor of the diocese; Father Fred Williams, a priest in charge at St. Stephen Church; and Bishop Julio Holguin (twenty months a bishop).

We discussed the Haitian refugee situation and were told that the Episcopal Church in the Dominican Republic works with refugees and that the work is supported by the bishop, who became even more sympathetic following the ouster of President Aristide.

From 1915 to the present, Haitians have been brought into the Dominican Republic to work in the sugar cane, rice, and coffee fields, as well as in construction. They also escaped into the Dominican Republic because of the desperate political and economic situation in their own country. Until the recent Haitian coup these refugees fled to the Dominican Republic to save their lives and escape Haitian tyranny, but upon entry nearly all were taken into the cane fields and forced to work.

Father Williams told us of a woman whose job was to go to the Haitian/Dominican border and recruit workers. She was paid 125 pesos for each person and the government gave her a truck and access to military personnel. She filled the truck with Haitians (including children) and brought them to the Dominican interior. Father Williams said the church was aware of the slave trade she was running at the time but remained silent because even church officials despised Haitians. He told us of his own indoctrination as a child when he was taught that Haitians "ate children."

In more recent years a United Nations group has coordinated a center for Haitian refugees, but the coordination has moved very slowly and the Dominican government even more slowly. Of the thousands of requests from Haitians for refugee status in the Dominican Republic, only 160 have been processed by the United Nations.

We were told of two Haitian priests and two deacons who go into the work camps to help refugees achieve legal status in the Dominican Republic. They also work to meet the educational and social needs of the people. Bishop Holguin estimates that there may be as many as 500 families in the camps that they serve.

The government of the Dominican Republic is undertaking a census as part of a process to repatriate many Haitian refugees. But a number of Dominican midwives have begun issuing Dominican birth certificates to Haitian babies, allowing them to be baptized as Dominicans. With all other groups of people, Dominican citizenship is automatically issued if their children are born in the country. Previously, Haitians often produced three generations not recognized as Dominican citizens. This allowed earlier Dominican administrations to use the lack of citizenship as an excuse for returning all Haitians below the age of seventeen and above the age of sixty, even though some of their children could not speak Creole. In 1991 the Episcopal Church's Committee on Ministry to Haitians challenged Dominican policy that Haitians born there could not be citizens.

As cheap Haitian labor became more available Dominicans working for ten to twenty pesos were replaced by Haitians willing to work the same number of hours for five pesos. The problem grew worse. In the 1970s the Episcopal Church was among those institutions that worked to expose the kidnapping of Haitian children and their forced labor under slave-like conditions.

We requested a meeting with the exiled Haitian ambassador to the Dominican Republic, Guy Alexander, who is also an anthropologist, sociologist, and former university professor.

He told us that the crisis in Haiti, which existed until the mid-1980s, was created by rulers who believed repression was necessary for the country to function. Ambassador Alexander said that social services have not been a part of the government for years but that up to the time of Aristide, that government consumed 40 percent of the national budget.

Aristide, he said, has become the person who can express what all oppressed groups in Haiti have been feeling. Today there is no system in place to support Aristide. Ambassador Alexander believes the present situation is aided by what he calls "the ambivalent attitude" of the United States toward Haiti.

Cuba Up Close
One of the most striking things one discovers upon entering Cuba is its isolation, most evidenced by the limited choices visitors have

of local restaurants, the inability of Cubans themselves to purchase basic necessities like deodorants, soap, toothpaste, Pampers, infant formula, and sanitary napkins.

Part of Cuba's extremity is a result of the blockade the United States has imposed; this leaves many Cuban people without medicine, food, or other essentials. Even the best homes had little or no toilet paper or soap and were without toilet seats. The collapse of socialism in the former Soviet Union has further contributed to Cuba's difficulty.

Much of the island is also ravaged from the recent storm that traveled up the eastern seaboard in March 1993.

In spite of hardships, the Cuban people were warm and embracing. Particularly moving was the sincere love and respect shown to African-Americans, even though there are tales in the U.S. of the country's caste system based upon skin color. Many told us Cuba is a country of mulattoes and that Cubans preoccupied with skin color have largely left the country.

We discovered that while medicine is unavailable to Cuban citizens, and food is in limited supply, tourists can eat well in certain hotels and restaurants and may purchase any articles they need. But long lines of Cubans can be seen waiting hours to purchase food outside a local grocery store with a meager selection.

The people we met made urgent appeals for an end to the U.S. embargo. The World and National Councils of Churches, and various denominations, have already done this and have sent tons of food and medicine into the country. The Episcopal Church has been part of this relief effort. We were reminded that U.S. senators have said they could not hold a dialogue with Cuba, but the people asked us how that is possible when the same senators held a dialogue with China while blood was still fresh in the streets of Tiananmen Square. And continuing dialogue is held with Nicaragua and El Salvador, they said, so why not with Cuba? They felt the answer is that they do not matter because they don't have enough of the products we need to make it worth our while to talk with them; they said they have no votes, no money, and little to trade. They point out that the Cubans we have welcomed in Miami are not supporters of Cuban socialism. One of the most serious concerns we heard regarding Cubans living in Miami is that upon their return to Cuba they will bring back the same racist tendencies they display in Miami that are "so typical of North America."

A number of our hosts pointed out that the U.S. blockade is aimed at Castro, but it has also denied aid to the Cuban people and that they look to us to be concerned about *human rights* in Cuba. Bishop Emillio Hernandez urged us as Christians to draw attention to what the blockade means to the people of Cuba, and to let the world know that bishops and priests are suffering along with their people because they feel it is their duty to be with the people.

The bishop was jailed for ten years for opposing Fidel Castro. He said he has never followed any man but Jesus Christ. He asked "where is the good will in the people" who don't want Cubans to have food and medicine? A Pentecostal woman lamented that it is "not right to bring a people to despair in order to change their ideas."

We went to the Martin Luther King, Jr. Center, which was opened in 1987. The group we met with was composed of two Baptist clergy (one woman and one man), a Pentecostal clergywoman, an Episcopal woman preparing for ordination, and an English woman who is a Quaker. There is pride in Cuba's African roots, and we were told that there is no sphere in Cuban life in which one cannot reach back to Africa.

The group told us that the economic situation has deteriorated in the last two years. The collapse of the former Soviet Union, the embargo, natural disasters (the March storm) that damaged the sugar crop, limited external trade, and errors of the Cuban government have all made meeting the needs of Cuban people difficult.

We were granted a meeting with Dr. Ricardo Alarcon, president of the National Assembly of Popular Power and former Cuban representative to the United Nations. He stressed that communication between the U.S. and Cuba must be based on mutual respect and international recognition.

After giving us some history of the relationship between Cuba and the U.S., dating back to Thomas Jefferson, Dr. Alarcon asked what possible threat Cuba could be to the U.S. following the disintegration of the U.S.S.R. He said this is a time when the embargo should be lifted, not tightened. He said that the only way Cubans can interpret the embargo is as a U.S. attempt to gain control of Cuba, as it attempted to do in the past. As others did before him, he pointed out that the embargo affects medicine and food—neither of which had anything to do with Cuba's former link with the Soviet Union. Because these are related to human needs, the people most seriously affected are mothers, children, and the elderly. He allowed that the Clinton presidency gives hope for a new and different type of relationship between Cuba and the U.S.A.

Neither the Batista nor Castro government has been able to solve problems of the common people, and in that regard Cuban people say they need to look at different governmental models. This year, for example, the country produced only 4 tons of sugar, as opposed to the 8 million it usually produces—all due to a lack of oil and the storm of the century. During the time we were there, the country expected a shipment of food and medicine from the Dominican Republic. This was destined first for schools, hospitals, jails, and homes for the elderly; anything left would go to other citizens.

Some of us had the opportunity to speak with a young man who is HIV positive. He told us that everyone who goes to the hospital for any ailment is tested for the AIDS virus and, if found to have it, is sent to live in sanitoriums where they receive the best food and medicine, free of charge. Interferon is produced in Cuba but AZT comes from outside the country. This young man appeared better fed than the elderly, young mothers, and children who are all well but unable to obtain food or needed medicine.

Episcopal Church work with HIV positive individuals began three years ago when people at Trinity Cathedral became aware of a case of AIDS outside the city. The ministry team is called Hope Community and now has forty members. We were told that homosexuality is not the kind of problem in Cuba that it appears to be in other places, and that people within the HIV/AIDS sanitorium are free to live as they choose.

We were told that if a man who is the breadwinner is moved to a sanitorium, he continues to receive his salary so that his family can be cared for. If he had been unemployed, the sanitorium gives enough money to have his family provided for. A small number of women are also in these sanitoriums.

In an unrelated health problem, over a six-month period 27,000 cases of blindness have been reported in Cuba. The government is spending an enormous amount of money trying to determine the cause. So far it has only affected people twenty-five years of age or older. Some people feel the blindness is the result of a vitamin deficiency.

Everyone we spoke with urged us to stress the need for dialogue in the U.S. concerning the fate of Cuba. U.S. churches continue to be urged to work for improved diplomatic relations, humanitarian aid, and to educate our people on the Cuban reality.

We left the country more aware than ever that the church must work to end the United States embargo of that tiny country, and bring it instead into the community of free nations.

An Intimate Encounter with Nicaragua

On June 9 we entered Managua, Nicaragua. We were met by Jorge Porter and Deacon Pedro Belige; Dr. Hernandez, president of the Nicaraguan Commission on Human Rights, was to have met with us, but the OAS, also meeting in Managua, preempted us.

We were taken to a meeting with Dr. Angelita Bahr, a German woman working with the Human Rights Commission for the last three years. Members told us that ten years ago the commission (Centro Nicaraguense de Derechos Humanos) was against the government. Today it remains independent; its status is similar to that of a nongovernmental organization (NGO).

Of all the Central American countries, Nicaragua has the fewest cases of AIDS. Commissioners stated that the first twenty-seven cases of AIDS involved foreigners; only eight to eleven cases involving Nicaraguans have been documented. Others in Nicaragua, however, estimate that numbers are much higher than reported.

We met later with Wilma Escosia, another human-rights advocate. She told us that there are three different human-rights organizations in Nicaragua. One was born in a struggle against the Contras. Another defends the civil and political rights of Nicaraguans, and the third attempts to see the government in a holistic way, which includes the old and new government, economic, social, cultural, peace, and environmental rights.

Three governmental departments respond to human-rights violation allegations. Most recently 162 persons have come forward with complaints and the numbers are growing each month. Ms. Escosia said that each report is investigated, whether it is finally substantiated or not.

The Department of Education also focuses on human-rights work and holds workshops in practical defense, while offering information on what each individual can do without a lawyer. Hunger strikes, demonstrations, and political organizing are typical foci at this department. The department also develops promoters of human rights who can prepare local communities by working with all levels of people, including field workers, base communities, farmers, and other NGOs. Often when this information is shared it is the first time people in the field realize that they have rights.

Much of the information is written in elementary forms for those who are not literate. For the literate, a human-rights case is published each week in a newsletter. A number of people want to develop a department of human rights for women as well as one for a healthy environment, but the timing depends on the right political atmosphere.

Between September 1991 and December 1992, 490 deaths were attributed to political human-rights violations—204 were said to be ex-Contras, 100 were of people from the fields and 70 were listed as Sandinistas or Sandinista sympathizers; 139 murders were recorded between January and March of 1993 in the northern area. Human-rights organizations hold the government responsible because it has not acted on these reported cases. The inefficiency of the government's judicial system in investigating reported violations has bred frustration.

The unemployment rate was reported to be as high as 55–60 percent and even 88 percent on Nicaragua's east coast. Unemployment is seen as a backdrop to increased sales of drugs, social disintegration, delinquency, prostitution, and violence against women and children.

Later in the day we met with Rosendo Diaz of the 1978 organization of Consejo Supremo de la Empresa Privada, which was created to oppose the Somoza government. Diaz spoke of illegal strikes and an atmosphere of anarchy, using as an analogy the expression that, "when a room is filled with water, the shortest people drown first." He said the U.S. is too eager to control the money it gives and that he fears evil will outlive good throughout the world because there are fewer and fewer good people.

On June 10 we met with Dr. Mateo Guerrero Flores of the Asociacion Nicaraguense Pro-Derechos Humanos, another human-rights organization. He said there have been eighty-five accusations of hidden cemeteries; the first five of those exhumed became part of ANPDH's early reports. Deaths in these cemeteries have been attributed to both the Contras and the Sandinistas. Forty-five people were similarly found near Bluefields in an open grave. Dr. Flores said he sees only good for the future because conditions can hardly get much worse than they are presently.

Our afternoon meeting was with Lic. Sergio D'Castro of the paper *Diario del F.S.L.N.* Lic. D'Castro said *Diario del F.S.L.N.* has allowed all segments of Nicaraguan society to express themselves and in this sense is in agreement with the present government. He said many avenues for solving problems should be open, but no solution to any problem will leave everyone satisfied; concessions will have to be made in order to allow all people to live together. In this regard he informed us of a recent meeting of Contra and Sandinista Mothers of the Disappeared who came together, realizing that they both suffer the loss of their children.

He said the first contribution that the U.S. can make is to respect Nicaragua because the country has been damaged by our policy of "meddling in [its] internal politics." The U.S. therefore has to take some responsibility for the problems existing in Nicaragua today and is morally obligated to help Nicaragua come out of the poverty it finds itself in. He said the U.S. owes Nicaragua $100 million in taxes and he admonished us saying, "one dollar used to destroy has a different effect than one dollar used to build up."

He said that when the U.S. speaks of democracy abroad it forgets that this is a new process in many countries, and that we (U.S. citizens) expect these countries to advance faster in a few short years than we advanced in 200 years. Nicaragua, he reminded us, has had only a generation of democracy.

On June 11 we had an audience with Presidenta Violetta Chamorro. She is dealing with a breakaway party that earlier helped put her in power. She described her duties and was gracious with all of us.

Later we met with Adam Morales and Emillio Porter of the Socialist party. They told us that the presidenta had established an alliance with the Sandinistas but that the people had voted for a change; this forced her to put aside that alliance. They attributed to this the present crisis in Nicaragua. They said, "Only in Nicaragua do those who win lose and those who lose win." The problem with the alliance, they continued, is that the electoral system, the army, the police, and functionaries of the government are Sandinistas and have sabotaged the action of the presidenta in favor of their own political interests. But the matter of property has not been solved; houses and farms that the Sandinistas illegally took over have not been returned to the landowners. They also denounced alleged violations of human rights by the police and army. They also charged that Presidenta Chamorro has appointed people to the assembly rather than allow for an election of representatives.

Emillio Porter is the youth representative to the Socialist party. He said he joined it because it is the party that cares about the young, and the young doubt that the presidenta really understands their problems.

When we asked how the church can help in Nicaragua, members of the party said it could by:

- maintaining relations with democratic organizations
- generating social projects in vulnerable sectors
- aiding agriculture
- respecting human-rights organizations
- giving "a helping hand"

The Reverend Ennis Duffis told us that of the 4 million people in Nicaragua about 3.5 million are poor. Therefore, he said, the United States needs to channel its financial assistance to poor people rather than send it to the Nicaraguan government. Father Duffis also reminded us that the 1988 General Convention of the U.S. Episcopal Church, meeting in Detroit, passed a resolution to raise $1.5 million for Latin America. Following that convention the executive council named the Presiding Bishop's Fund for World Relief as administrator of the fund. To date, none of the money has been received in Latin America.

Duffis said it is difficult for the presidenta to find a solution to problems because business people do not have confidence in her ability to create new jobs. To the surprise of many who thought she would be only a figurehead, she began to run Nicaragua herself following her election. Father Duffis feels this has left many feeling "betrayed" because they cannot control her.

In a meeting on the lawn of the diocesan offices, Episcopal Bishop Downs spoke of the 56–60 percent unemployment rate, but he also said there are more millionaires now than during the time of Somoza; there is still a clear division between rich and poor. He also spoke of recent fires that were set in tobacco fields because the farmers were of a different political persuasion from the arsonists.

We asked him what the country needed. The first thing, he said, was stability, followed by the creation of jobs. The largest part of the population are farmers, many seeking an international market by growing nontraditional crops.

The presidenta is not really the presidenta, Bishop Downs told us, and went on to say that her son-in-law (Antonio Lacallo) is everything. (This confirmed our evaluation of our meeting with her in which her son-in-law did most of the responding to the more serious political questions we raised.) The bishop also spoke of her involvement with the Roman Catholic Church which, he told us, is the only organization exempt from paying taxes.

Owing to our meeting with Presidenta Chamorro we were unable to meet with the mothers of the heroes and martyrs as we had planned to do that afternoon.

Adding up the total picture in the country, we found that in the 1980s, the U.S. was unyielding in its determination to undermine the economic and political stability of Nicaragua. Following decades of earlier interventions, our government committed millions of dollars to overt and covert efforts to unseat a duly elected government. Since the 1990 election of Dona Violetta Chamorro, we found that Nicaragua continues to be plagued by unemployment, rampant inflation, and political instability.

Many told us that Dona Violetta remains a figurehead president, with her son-in-law, Antonio Lacallo, as *de facto* chief of state. The Sandinista presence is still strong, which is seriously questioned by both the right and the left. The U.S. has not released all the promised USAID money that might help "jump-start" the failing economy. Nicaragua has become the second poorest country in the hemisphere.

Many in Nicaragua regard the current government as corrupt and inefficient. While the return of private property was promised, officials have not kept those promises. Land was confiscated from the Somoza regime by the Sandinistas who created cooperative farm ventures. As they left power, they were permitted to gain title to much of the socialized land. Now, land fraud has resulted in much property finding its way to the Chamorro family.

Nicaragua needs capital infusion to provide an adequate economic program. Export of natural resources—wood and shellfish in particular—is failing to create employment opportunities and is ruining the fragile ecology. Drug trafficking is increasing and social disintegration is apparent among the indigenous Miskito people of the Atlantic Coast.

The constitution mandates health care, education, and social security for all at government expense, but because the government cannot fund those services, the people are being charged for them. Lack of adequate medication and sanitation have made cholera and other diseases endemic. The highly successful literacy campaign of the Sandinista government has been abandoned, and many children are not in school because of the new costs.

Military courts have precedence over civil courts. Few justices have been replaced since the Sandinista days. The disarming of the Contras and local militia has not been accomplished. Many human-rights abuses are cited, and the national security police remain in control in the countryside. Constitutional guarantees against search and seizure have been suspended, which gives the police inordinate power. The hope for change following the election has not materialized for the *campesinos*; costs have risen exponentially and land is not available. The country needs to be politically and socially stabilized.

The work of the Episcopal Church in Nicaragua is primarily in Managua and on the Pacific Coast. It facilitates social programs within the vulnerable social sectors and speaks out on human-rights abuses in a new atmosphere of free speech.

■　■　■

Altogether, in these four countries, we found the mission and ministry of the Episcopal Church centered on concern for the *campesinos*, providing social services, and exposing human-rights abuses. Humanitarian support from the larger Episcopal Church is needed in the Caribbean and Central America. The U.S. church should continue to be concerned with these countries, to be sure help is directed to them and to inform North Americans about our brothers and sisters to our south.

At home we should do all we can to engage Christians with the assumptions and implications of nationalism, racism, greed, and ignorance, all focused in the rhetoric of Manifest Destiny, and all suspect in the light of sufferings of the poor in Central America, the Caribbean, and the Philippines.

DISCUSSION QUESTIONS

1. Would U.S. Manifest Destiny thinking appeal to you if you had been born south of the Rio Grande?

2. Does race play a role in U.S. foreign policy or military commitments?
3. Is the U.S. really responsible for any of the difficulties experienced by poor people in the countries named in this chapter? For the wealth or position of the privileged in these countries?
4. How do you understand the ministry of the local churches in the countries studied?
5. What insights might be gained from this chapter concerning new mission priorities for the U.S. churches?
6. Are the poor in foreign countries in any important sense our neighbors?
7. In light of the present chapter, evaluate the proposition that religion and politics are never finally separable.
8. What are some practical actions that could be taken at the local congregational level to help people become more informed about churches in other countries?

CONCLUSION

I n the introduction to this work, I tried to sketch an outline of a
Christian social ethics–based notion of faithful leadership, which
could be differentiated in its assumptions, goals, and driving
force from economics-based or psychology-based leadership theories
of the day. In particular I posited the need to recover the biblical
accents of peace and justice, and the need to recognize that formal
leaders, at any rate, are usually in positions to tilt social organizations slightly toward, or away from, these emphases.

I proposed that all Christians should see themselves as influencers
of formal leaders, by being critics and advocates regarding decisions
made in the leadership arena; in this presumption is our tacit recognition that even we ourselves are leaders. This presumption should
be heartily affirmed—precisely in the sense in which Jesus coun-
seled his disciples not to hide their light under a bushel. (Even
apart from Christian notions, in our democracy the government is
"of, by, and for" the people; we are all supposed to be active, to be
leaders in this sense.) A Christian familiar with the Bible, moreover,
can usefully be guided in leadership matters. A way in which the
Bible tests whether some degree or other of divine peace and justice
is present in the land is by evaluating the prospects of the people
at the bottom of the social order.

Despite the way we think things should work, certain familiar
influences buffet formal leaders, one of the most telling of which is
that in a democracy they must respond primarily to the interests
of their constituencies. For all practical purposes this means an
economically privileged constituency. Such a circumstance inclines
formal leadership to decisions favoring those at the top. But if injustice oppresses the weak, Christians should insist that right be done.
The Bible discloses that the cause of the least becomes God's cause
whenever there is injustice and violence; if their prospects are auspi-

cious in society, there is a goodly portion of divine justice and peace in the land, and if not auspicious, there is not.

We intuitively know that we need a more just and peaceable world. Societal influences and ordinary self-interest, however, have diverted us from doing the good that we should, while they have beguiled us into doing what we should not. The Apostle Paul would not be surprised at our condition, nor St. Augustine. The suffering caused by this social distortion is considerable, particularly among the poor in our land and elsewhere where our nation has been implicated, so again we need to focus the leadership issue from the viewpoint of the vulnerable. Formal leaders should be held accountable to the justice and peace requirements of the Christian tradition, while all Christians must in some way appropriate to themselves leadership responsibilities, whether they fill formal leadership positions or not.

The tough mind and tender heart formulation of Martin Luther King, Jr., is apt today, the more so when the former is put in the service of the latter. But there is a need for caution against our own assumptions and willfulness in thinking we know the precise will of God. The best we can hope for is an indication based upon scripture study, scrutiny of the Christian heritage, and the insights of Christian community.

The range of practical leadership tasks may run from riskful demonstration of Christ's nonviolent and inclusive love, to a selfless zeal to protect, warn, and nurture the vulnerable. The active peace- and justice-advocacy implications of these sorts of commitments are considerable for a society grinding along today in apparent indifference to God and to the marginalized in our own country and abroad.

Spirituality, for the present purpose, refers to our inner disposition to exercise leadership consistent with the patterns suggested above. This requires a high degree of honesty and clarity in daring to read the world's suffering reality. If we don't actually see this pain, and in some degree feel it, then our witnessing and watching would likely be only a gesture. We need to keep an eye on the powerful, the pretentious, and the presumed best and brightest, for we know from history—especially the Manifest Destiny phase—both the good and also the very bad things of which all are capable. To dispose ourselves thus warily is an inconvenience, to put it mildly, and there are well-known dangers resembling tendencies to paranoia. But what I mean is not that; rather it is a willingness to see, as Orwell, for instance, determined to see how it is for people in difficulty, and to be appropriately responsible.

Our spirituality is developed within the framework of our Christian faith that the same God who wants us to be concerned with peace-and-justice issues is the God who forgives—forgives us and everyone. Knowing this, we are delivered from a psychology of fanaticism. The lightness of our spiritual being thus engendered is not the rootless emptiness described by Kundera in his well-known novel, but a way of not taking ourselves or our mission with dreadful seriousness.

There is a need to avoid the phony spirituality of passivity for its own sake, self-absorption, or alternatively an escape into perseverating fanaticism. The right kind of witness to God's caring is needed by all of us, but it is needed in leaders particularly. What the Bible calls "purity of heart" implies a tenacity in keeping on with faithful tasks in pursuit of the good. Immersion in the events of the world is essential, since there is hardly any other place we could be— which is usually acknowledged as a fact of physics but not necessarily as a datum of spirituality. A faithful, mature, witnessing spirituality in our era implies courage and love.

The key to an appropriate response from Christian people (=Christian leaders; all of us) lies in the infinite importance we attach to each individual life, as did Jesus. This helps us watch and warn of collective social tendencies, policies, and practices that devalue individuals or minority groups—usually on a social-utility basis. That is, Christian leadership watches out for the tyranny of the self-designated "normal" majority, who may indulge an unexamined eugenics type of bias in finding ill or disabled people unworthy of full regard, protection, and support. Especially when ill people are members of another socially devalued group—a racial minority, the homeless, etc.—there is all the more need to make the justice case, and make it stick. Christian leadership in this context witnesses positively to the importance of each *one*, regardless. This insight is the essential and perhaps unique theological contribution needed so urgently from Christians in our churches and society today.

For Christians, an enormous theological issue is, who or what is God: the nation or Jesus Christ? Subsumed under this are other religious questions: Are we, or are we not, called to love others described to us as our enemies? Are we in fact reconciled to all others, because of Christ's redemptive act and his grace? Do we, or do we not, look out into this treacherous world from the foot of the cross—i.e., from the standpoint of war's victims? Have we conceded to the military the language of personal honor and courage, or do we yet insist upon its Christian connotations? Is suspending our Christian ethics–based critical acuity, in compliance with the official version of hate thy enemy, a harmless exercise, or is it bad faith? Is it a modern form of spiritual apostasy? Inherent in these questions, depending upon how we answer them, is an emerging pressure for all faithful Christians to come to maturity: to watch and witness, and that, in this or any era, implies courage and love.

Christians have to be alert to the dubious motives of political and industry leaders, and respectful of the public's too-easy acceptance of a designated external enemy. For example, we don't need to "stand tall," because if we ever really needed such a thing Jesus has already stood tall for us—and for the Iraqis too, whether or not that is acknowledged in Baghdad or Washington. Witness is needed too concerning the uselessness of the just war theory and its cynical manipulation for propaganda purposes by our elected leadership. Witness could have been made that from a Christian point of view, being a bully boy in the world yields no good in the long run; as a nation we were on more solid ground, with ourselves and with other nations, when out of a prudent generosity we developed the Marshall Plan—*before* it was cynically sold to the people of the U.S. for its anti-Soviet utility.

Christian people—that is, Christians operating in responsible recognition of their need to play a strong leadership role in this fragile world—need to think, speak, and act if there is to be any hope of breaking our national enthrallment to war. Christians need to remember, and keep alive the memory, of incredible suffering in Iraq; this is suffering for which our nation is primarily responsible. A witnessing function along this line will get us nowhere with the powers that be, but as Santayana first said, if we don't remember the past, we are condemned to repeat it. And from a religious perspective, there is the crucial matter that repentance is essential to the soul's health; it usually requires contrition, and contrition implies a consciousness of the injury that has been done in the first place. Repeating the blood-stained past, unfortunately from a learning point of view, has been easy for us because, by and large, as a nation we have not yet suffered much from war.

Christians ought to watch for war and arms-profit addiction as carefully as we watch for cancer or heart disease. Watching must be tireless for weapons-worship, demonizing some external group, and propagandizing. We have to accord the fullest respect for the power of war and profits to capture our hearts, minds, and souls. In this sense, war and greed are the ultimate demonstration of the devil. Witness, simultaneously with watching, must effectively be made to the sovereignty of Christ and Christ's Kingdom—to the preeminence of forgiving, forbearing, tolerating, seeking to understand and to reconcile because ultimately we are already reconciled; above all, witnessing must show what it means to be steadfastly faithful to God. Can there be today any more noble calling for us than this?

The nuclear phenomenon, more than any other, characterizes the world in which we all must live together today. With the Three Mile Island incident, then overwhelmingly after Chernobyl, public skepticism has increased in our country concerning the veracity of official industry and government leaders. With this specific alarm has occurred a correspondingly generalized erosion in overall public trust in nuclear affairs. When a process of doubting and mistrust gets underway the intangible social bonds necessary to hold a community together become strained, and they may ultimately break. The end of this process would be the disappearance of any reasonable prospects for a just and peaceable society. Official secrecy and deceit thus pose a serious problem for Christians.

We can become more jaded and cynical than we admit even to ourselves—most of all when we suspect contempt for ordinary folks in the arrogant pursuit of their own programs by the ruthless and greedy few; subtly we can be rendered helpless, passive, and despairing in the face of the monolith. Against this, the case must always be made that trust-engendering truth-telling is essential on the part of our formal leaders. Witness is needed concerning the rightful place of technology as a servant of people, not as their potential violator. It is needed today as much as was Martin Luther's confidence-building assertion of several centuries ago, that "though this world with devils filled should threaten to undo us, we will not fear, for God has willed his truth to triumph through us." We dare to hope that one day we will learn to develop, apply, and control technologies that are not too big for us, and that a way will be found to use them safely, confidently, openly, and honestly—for everyone.

The U.S. arms trade is impossible to approve, unless we are benefitting from it personally or we accept the incorrect claim that it
helps our economy. Plainly it does not. The humane approach is to
undertake a deliberate, planned process of economic conversion,
overcoming the addiction to short-term gain, and establishing a new
foundation for socially useful production. The proper response to
"If we don't sell arms, others will" is to work for a humane way to
control all such sales, or if needs be, to say, "Let them, but as for
us: No."

Our commission's various investigations into countries previously
(presently?) regarded as the pawns of divinely mandated U.S. de-
signs enabled us to see the tangible consequences of racism, indifference, misguided messianism, and self-aggrandizement that
undoubtedly occur throughout the entire human species. The purpose of our inquiry was not to build a moral case against the U.S.,
but instead to awaken U.S. churches and our government to certain
responsibilities, however immediate or historically remote.

Patently we can live our lives without having to worry about Cuba
or the mountains of northern Luzon; we learned, though, that the
people in those countries watch *us* like hawks. They have, wholesale,
immense faith in the goodness of "the average American." My claim
is that Christianly informed leadership entails a sincere regard for
folks like these and a commensurate dedication to their welfare.
After all, Christians believe most deeply in love, and the greatest
love is the least self-interested—which means caring about people
we will never meet and who are not positioned to do anything in
return for us. There is an aspect of the Divine in this, which we
believe is but an intimation of the Glory that is to be revealed to
all people.

■ ■ ■

My friend Harmon Smith, at Duke University's Divinity School,
relates a story told to him by the Lutheran pastor Reger, once an
inmate at Dachau. Pointing to the *priesterbarraks* that once housed
faithful Christians in an appalling time, Reger said to Smith: "Where
there is no risk, there is no commitment; where there is no commitment, there is no witness; where there is no witness, there is no
hope; and where there is no hope, there is no gospel."

This book has been but a stammering hymn to Reger.

NOTES

INTRODUCTION

1. Arthur Meier Schlesinger, Jr., *A Thousand Days* (Boston: Houghton Mifflin, 1965), ch. 37. Quoted in John Bartlett, *Bartlett's Familiar Quotations* (Boston: Little, Brown and Company, 1980), p. 894.

2. J. Edward Carothers, in *The Paralysis of Mainstream Protestant Leadership* (Nashville: Abingdon Press, 1990), p. 80, says, "A sure sign of paralysis is when leadership begins to make more and more of ritual, tradition, finery of symbols, and special attractions."

3. James R. Wood has studied the gap between parish clergy and their congregations that existed in the 1970s on issues of social concern. His study is with largely middle-class, "mainstream" parishes in Indianapolis. The work is contained in *Leadership in Voluntary Organizations: The Controversy over Social Action in the Protestant Churches* (New Brunswick: Rutgers University Press, 1981).

4. See David Ray Griffin, ed., *Spirituality and Society: Postmodern Visions* (Albany: State University of New York Press, 1988). See also David Ray Griffin, William A. Beardslee, and Joe Holland, *Varieties of Postmodern Theology* (Albany: State University of New York Press, 1989). It will become clear that for my present purpose, the marks of a postmodern world, in contrast to a modern world, are the useful thoughts in these books; I do not appropriate the process theology with which they are closely intertwined.

5. Griffin, *Spirituality and Society*, p. 36.

6. Ibid., p. 85.

7. Griffin, Beardslee, and Holland, *Varieties of Postmodern Theology*, p. 2.

8. Ibid., p. 2.

9. Griffin, *Spirituality and Society*, pp. 3ff.

10. Ibid., p. ix.

11. Carter Heyward does an interesting job on restructuring the Jesus of history versus Christ of faith debate in *Speaking of Christ* (New York: The Pilgrim Press, 1989), pp. 13–22.

12. "Question Man," by Conti. *San Francisco Chronicle*. I have lost the date and page number.

13. Karl Barth, whose theological views are not otherwise presented in this book, emphasized the importance of Christian witness. He held that the church's job was to witness beyond itself to God and Christ, particularly in showing that reconciliation is a fact already accomplished by God for all people. (*Church Dogmatics* IV/3, Preface, pp. xif, 554ff, 762ff, 795ff and 830ff, and *Church Dogmatics* IV/1, pp. 725ff.)

JUSTICE AND ILL PEOPLE

1. Irving Cooper, *Living with Chronic Neurologic Disease* (New York: Norton, 1976), p. 35.
2. James Jones, *World War II* (New York: Ballantine Books, 1975), p. 88.
3. Simone Weil, *Waiting for God*. Trans. by Emma Crawford (New York: Harper and Row, 1973).
4. Cheri Register, *Living with Chronic Illness* (New York: The Free Press, 1988).
5. Stephen Schmidt, "Living with Chronic Illness: Why Should I Go On?" *The Christian Century* (May 3, 1989), p. 475.
6. John Updike, "The City," *Trust Me* (New York: Random House, 1987), p. 37.
7. Jonathan Cott, *Visions and Voices* (New York: Dolphin/Doubleday, 1987).
8. Clifton Fadiman, *Anecdotes* (Boston: Little, Brown, 1985), p. 502.
9. Krister Stendahl in *Interpretation* (Fall 1980).
10. Nancy Mairs, *Plaintext* (Tucson: University of Arizona Press, 1986), p. 7.
11. Robert F. Murphy, *The Body Silent* (New York: Henry Holt, 1987), p. 66.
12. David Baumann, "Remembering Joseph Carey Merrick," *The Living Church* (August 5, 1990).
13. Douglas Martin, "Some People Only Look Skin Deep," *The New York Times* (January 16, 1991).
14. Woody Guthrie, *Bound for Glory* (New York: E. P. Dutton, 1968), p. 117.
15. Joe Klein, *Woody Guthrie: A Life* (New York: Knopf, 1980), p. 429.
16. Alan Blum, "Yellow Nicotine Stains on Blue Collars," *Washington Post National Weekly Edition* (June 16, 1986), p. 24.
17. "The January Almanac," *The Atlantic* (Jan. 1991), p. 20.
18. Elisabeth Rosenthal, "Health Problems of Inner City Poor Reach Crisis Point," *The New York Times* (December 24, 1990), p. 1.
19. Ibid.
20. Ibid., p. 9.
21. Ibid.
22. Ibid.
23. Ibid.
24. Milton Freudenheim, "Health Care a Growing Burden," *The New York Times* (January 29, 1991), p. C-1.
25. Ibid.
26. Susan Parker, "The Basics of Health Care," *Sojourners* (Dec. 1990), p. 32.
27. The University of California, Berkeley, *Wellness Letter*, 7:5 (February 1, 1991), p. 1.

28. See Timothy Egan, "Oregon Shakes up Pioneering Health Plan for the Poor," *The New York Times* (February 22, 1991), p. A-11.

29. Robert Hood, *Social Teachings of the Episcopal Church* (Wilton, CT: Morehouse, 1990), p. 140.

30. Leonard A. Sagan, *The Health of Nations* (New York: Basic Books, 1987). See especially Chapter Six, "Stress, Resilience, and the Hopelessness-Helplessness Syndrome," pp. 111–128.

THE CHURCH AND THE PLIGHT OF CHILDREN

1. Canticles Rabbah. Quoted in *Welcoming the Child* (Washington, D.C.: Children's Defense Fund, 1991), p. 5.

2. *Welcoming the Child*, p. 14.

3. Hilary Putnam, *Realism with a Human Face* (Cambridge: Harvard University Press, 1990), p. 149.

4. Much of the information in this section is drawn from "Notes in the History of Childhood," by Henry F. Smith, MD, published in *Harvard Magazine* (July-August 1984), pp. 62c–65g.

5. John Boswell, *The Kindness of Strangers* (New York: Pantheon, 1990).

6. *The Christian Science Monitor* (September 20, 1990), p. 10.

7. Joyce Hollyday, "Giving Children 'First Call,'" *Sojourners* (December 1990); also the editors, *The Nation* (December 18, 1989).

8. Hollyday, ibid.

9. James Agee and Walker Evans, *Let Us Now Praise Famous Men* (New York: Ballantine, 1974), p. 266.

10. Seth Mydans, "Homicide Rate for Young Blacks Rose by Two-Thirds in Five Years," *New York Times* (December 7, 1990).

11. Richard Louv, *Childhood's Future* (Boston: Houghton-Mifflin, 1990).

12. Eileen Simpson, *Orphans* (New York: Weidenfeld and Nicolson, 1987).

13. John Cheever, "Growing Up in the Fifties," *The New Yorker* (August 13, 1990), p. 32.

14. Joseph Berger, "Nursery Schools Resist I.Q. Test for 4-Year-Olds," *New York Times* (December 26, 1990).

15. Shann Nix, "Looking Up to the Stars," *San Francisco Chronicle* (June 26, 1989).

16. Jill Krementz, *How It Feels When a Parent Dies* (New York: Knopf, 1986), pp. 35, 75.

17. Wyatt Prunty, "Learning the Bicycle," *The American Scholar* (Winter, 1989), p. 122.

18. Lewis Smedes, *Mere Morality: What God Expects from Ordinary People* (Grand Rapids: Eerdmans, 1983), p. 83f.

19. Quoted in Robert Coles, *The Call of Stories* (Boston: Little, Brown, 1986), p. 183.

PEACEMAKING MINISTRY IN BELLIGERENT TIMES

1. Thomas Powers, commentary in *The Atlantic* (August 1987).

2. Chris Hedges, "War Is Vivid in Gun Sights of the Sniper," *New York Times* (February 3, 1991), p. 1.

3. Kate Millet, *et al. New York Times* (January 20, 1991).

4. Laura Palmer, *Shrapnel in the Heart* (New York: Random House, 1987), p. 42.

5. E. L. Doctorow, "Open Letter to the President," *The Nation* (January 7/14, 1991), p. 6.

6. Jack Newfield, *The Village Voice*. [I have lost the date of this issue.]

7. David Cornwell, "The Clandestine Muse," *The Johns Hopkins Magazine* (August 1990).

8. Philip Hallie, *Lest Innocent Blood Be Shed* (New York: Harper and Row, 1979), p. 104.

9. Ibid., p. 285.

10. Charles Peguy, *The Mystery of the Charity of Joan of Arc* (Manchester, U.K.: Carcanet, 1986), pp. 38–39.

11. Arnold Toynbee, "The Reluctant Death of Sovereignty," *Center Magazine* (March 1968), pp. 29, 33.

12. Quoted in Theodore Draper, "The True History of the Gulf War," *New York Review of Books* (January 30, 1992), p. 40. Understanding the larger historical context of the region is crucial to a correct understanding of the forces at work there in the first place. A brief, highly readable historical account is given in Theodore Draper, "The Gulf War Reconsidered," *The New York Review of Books* (January 16, 1992), pp. 46–53. An excellent presentation of the entire situation and its history is given in *Lines in the Sand: Justice and the Gulf War*, by Alan Geyer and Barbara G. Green (Louisville: Westminster/John Knox Press, 1992).

13. Draper, "True History," p. 40.

14. Ibid., p. 41.

15. Ibid.

16. Ibid.

17. Ibid.

18. Ibid. See his footnote 29.

19. Ibid.

20. Ibid.

21. The editors, *In These Times* (January 15–21, 1992), p. 14. Alan Geyer reports that Iraq itself had been a U.S. arms customer: "From 1985 to 1990, the U.S. sold Iraq $1.5 billion worth of military equipment and high technology items." This was done out of U.S. antipathy to Iran, Iraq's enemy. Geyer identifies Hewlett-Packard, Hughes Aircraft, and Bell Aerospace as particularly rewarded by military-equipment sales to Iraq during this time. (Geyer, p. 49.)

22. *In These Times*, p. 14.

23. David Albright and Mark Hibbs, "Iraq's Bomb: Blueprints and Artifacts," *Bulletin of the Atomic Scientists* (January/February 1992), pp. 30–40.

24. See Garry Emmons, "Did PR Firm Invent Gulf War Stories?" *In These Times* (January 22–28, 1992), p. 2.

25. Russell F. Sizemore, "Reflections on the Gulf War," *The Christian Century* (January 15, 1992), p. 46.

26. David S. Cunningham, "Resurrection in the Wake of War," *Christianity and Crisis* (October 7, 1991).

27. Draper, "True History," p. 41.

28. Len Ackland, "Democracy for Kuwait?" *Bulletin of the Atomic Scientists* (October 1991), p. 2.

29. Draper, "True History," p. 39.

30. Richard Golob, "Kuwait: A Progress Report," *Harvard Magazine* (January-February 1992), p. 129.

31. Draper, "True History," p. 44.

32. Quoted in Draper, "True History," p. 40.

33. Michael T. Klare, "High-Death Weapons of the Gulf War," *The Nation* (June 3, 1991), p. 721.

34. Ibid. p. 742.

35. Ibid.

36. *New York Times* (March 23, 1991). Quoted in Draper, "True History," p. 40.

37. Judy Devlin, "Testimony Before the House Select Committee on Hunger" (November 13, 1991). Quoted in Draper, "True History," p. 40.

38. Susan Sachs, "UN Scales Back Forecast of Iraqi Infant Death Toll," *Philadelphia Inquirer* (July 11, 1991), p. 12. Quoted in George A. Lopez, "The Gulf War: Not So Clean," *Bulletin of the Atomic Scientists* (September 1991), p. 32.

39. Devlin, in Draper, "True History," p. 40.

40. Interview: Dr. Tim Cote, "A Tragic Year Later: Infant Mortality in Post War Iraq," *Sojourners* (January 1992).

41. Tim McDermott, "Testimony before the House Select Committee on Hunger." Quoted in Draper, "True History," p. 40.

42. James Fine, "Oil Sale Would Ease Iraq's Health Crisis," *The Christian Century* (January 15, 1992), p. 36f.

43. "Damage in Iraq Worse than Meant," *The San Francisco Sunday Examiner and Chronicle* (February 23, 1992), p. A-4.

44. Sizemore, *Reflections on the Gulf War*, p. 48.

45. Lopez, *The Gulf War*, p. 35.

46. Editors, *The Nation* (February 3, 1992), p. 112.

47. Draper, "True History," p. 43.

48. Ibid. p. 45.

49. Jean Bethke Elshtain, "Just War and American Politics," *The Christian Century* (January 15, 1992), p. 44.

50. Draper, "True History," p. 44.

51. E. L. Doctorow, "War Torn," *Mirabella* (May 1991), p. 50.

52. Draper, "True History," p. 45, quotes *The Weekly Compilation of Presidential Documents* (March 8, 1991), p. 284.

53. Draper, "True History," p. 45.

54. Eduard Lohse, *Theological Ethics of the New Testament*. Trans. by Eugene Boring (Minneapolis: Fortress Press, 1991), p. 56f.

55. Elshtain, *Just War*, p. 42.

56. Michael S. Gordon, "2 Ex-Military Chiefs Urge Bush to Delay Gulf War," *New York Times* (November 29, 1990), p. 1.

57. Barton Gellman, "U.S. Bombs Missed 70% of Time," *The Washington Post* (March 16, 1991), p. A1.

58. Walzer is quoted in Sizemore, *Reflections on the Gulf War*, p. 46.

59. Quoted in Lopez, *The Gulf War*, p. 34. Alan Geyer writes, "The devastation of bridges and other escape routes, the clogging of miles of highways, and the coalition strategy of envelopment made retreat an impossibility for many divisions of Iraqi troops in Kuwait and southern Iraq. Surrender was a possibility only for some of these; slaughter was the fate of others. (p. 140.)

60. Lopez, *The Gulf War*, p. 34.

61. Elshtain, *Just War*, p. 43.

62. The Rt. Rev. Samir Kafity, "A Message of Peace." Letter from Jerusalem dated August 21, 1990.

63. Edmond L. Browning, presiding bishop and primate, "A Statement to Episcopalians by the Presiding Bishop on the Persian Gulf Crisis, October 5, 1990" (New York: Episcopal News Service).

64. *The Christian Century* (December 5, 1990), p. 1127. See also *New York Times* (November 16, 1990), p. A-10. An impressive collection of NCC statements on the Gulf War (*Pressing for Peace*) is available from the NCC Middle East Office, 475 Riverside Drive, Room 612, New York, New York 10115.

65. *The Christian Century*, (December 5, 1990), p. 1127.

SOCIETAL INTEGRITY AND OFFICIAL DECEIT

1. David Grossman, "Neo-Luddites: Don't Just Say Yes to Technology," *Utne Reader* (March/April 1990), p. 44.

2. Grigori Medvedev, *The Truth About Chernobyl*. Trans. by Evelyn Rossiter (New York: Basic Books, 1990), p. 161.

3. Chart: "Axis of Fear," from *The Emergency Public Relations Manual* (Pase, Incorporated). The chart is reprinted in *Harper's* (May 1989), p. 31.

4. Francis X. Clines, "Chernobyl Cleanup Leads to Charge," *New York Times International* (February 8, 1991), p. A-3.

5. Gabriel Schoenfeld, "A Dosimeter for Every Dacha," *Bulletin of the Atomic Scientists* (July/August 1989), p. 13.

6. See Medvedev, *The Truth About Chernobyl*.

7. Karl Z. Morgan, "Ways of Reducing Radiation Exposure in a Future Nuclear Power Economy," *Nuclear Power Safety*, ed. by James H. Rust and Lynn E. Weaver (New York: Pergamon Press, 1976), pp. 156, 160–162. Quoted in Medvedev, *The Truth*, p. 266.

8. David Albright, "Chernobyl and the U.S. Nuclear Industry," *Bulletin of the Atomic Scientists* (November 1986), p. 38.

9. Shannon Fagan, "Steve Comley, NRC Enemy," *In These Times* (September 11–17, 1991), p. 4f.

10. Albright, "Chernobyl," p. 38.

11. Matthew L. Wald, "A-Plant To Close Over Safety Issue," *New York Times* (October 2, 1991), p. A-1.

12. "Westinghouse Admits Goofs at A-Plants," *San Francisco Chronicle* (November 14, 1988), p. A-11.

13. Jim Connor, "Nuclear Workers at Risk," *Bulletin of the Atomic Scientists* (September 1990), pp. 25–28.

14. Ibid.

15. Robert Gillette, "Radiation Studies Are Still Inconclusive," *This World* (November 20, 1988), pp. 19–21.

16. Bryan Abas, "Rocky Flats: A Big Mistake from Day One," *Bulletin of the Atomic Scientists* (December 1989), p. 24.

17. Jay Olshansky and Gary Williams, "Culture Shock at the Weapons Complex," *Bulletin of the Atomic Scientists* (September 1990), p. 29.

18. Jim Rice, "Mistakes Were Made . . . ," *Sojourners* (January, 1991), p. 33.

19. Gabriel Schoenfeld, "Rad Storm Rising," *The Atlantic* (December 1990), p. 54.

20. John F. Ahearne, "Telling the Public About Risks," *Bulletin of the Atomic Scientists* (September 1990), p. 39.

21. Harvey Wasserman, "Chernobyl's Deadly Legacy," *Utne Reader* (May/June 1990),. p. 30.

22. Editorial, *The Nation* (April 10, 1989), p. 471.

23. Ibid.

24. The Editors, *Sojourners* (January 1991).

25. Ahearne, "Telling the Public," p. 39.

26. William Arkin and Joshua Handler, "Nuclear Disasters at Sea, Then and Now," *Bulletin of the Atomic Scientists* (July/August 1989), p. 24.

27. Ibid.

28. Reported in David Holloway, "The Catastrophe and After," *New York Review of Books* (July 19, 1990), p. 5.

29. Ibid.

30. Medvedev, *The Truth*, p. 72f.

31. Ibid., p. 132.

32. Ahearne, "Telling the Truth," p. 37.

33. Associated Press, "Soviets Ask for Help in Coping with Chernobyl," *Marin* [California] *Independent Journal* (April 28, 1990), p. A-4.

34. Felicity Barringer, "Chernobyl: Five Years Later the Danger Persists," *New York Times Magazine* (April 14, 1991), p. 36.

35. Ahearne, "Telling the Truth," p. 37f.

36. Ibid., p. 39.

37. Medvedev, *The Truth*, p. 259.

38. Zhores A. Medvedev, *Nuclear Disaster in the Urals* (New York: Norton, 1979).

39. "Soviets Admit to '57 Radioactive Blast," *San Francisco Chronicle* (June 17, 1989), p. A-12.

40. John May, *The Greenpeace Book of the Nuclear Age* (New York: Pantheon Books, 1989), pp. 119–123.

41. *The New Yorker* (May 6, 1991), p. 32.

42. "U.S. Vows to End A-Plant Secrecy," *San Francisco Chronicle* (June 17, 1989), p. A-7.

43. Editors: "In Brief: Just Don't Use the N-Word," *Bulletin of the Atomic Scientists* (May 1991), p. 6.

44. Connor, "Nuclear Workings," p. 25.

45. Editors, "Human Guinea Pigs," *Bulletin of the Atomic Scientists* (September 1990), p. 2.

46. Karen Dorn Steele, "Tracking Down Hanford's Victims," *Bulletin of the Atomic Scientists* (October 1990), p. 7.

47. Matthew Wald, "New Setbacks for Nuclear Arms Complex," *New York Times* (September 20, 1991), p. A-10.

48. Brian Jaudon, "In the Shadow of the Bomb," *Sojourners* (January 1989), p. 5.

49. Dick Russell, "In the Shadow of the Bomb," *The Amicus Journal* (Fall 1990), p. 25.

50. Jack Horan, "Latest Scram at Savannah Reactors," *Bulletin of the Atomic Scientists* (December 1988), p. 8.

51. Connor, "Nuclear Workers," p. 27.

52. Russell, "In the Shadow," p. 26.

53. Sissela Bok, *Lying: Moral Choice in Public and Private Life* (New York: Vintage, 1978), p. 30.

54. Ibid, p. 204.

55. Sissela Bok, *Secrets: On the Ethics of Concealment and Revelation* (New York: Vintage, 1983), p. 18.

56. Bok, *Secrets*, p. 285.

57. Ibid., p. 172.

58. Ibid., p. 181.

59. Maya Angelou, *All God's Children Need Traveling Shoes* (New York: Random House, 1986), p. 207.

60. I have been unable to locate the source for this quote. It appears in a collection of quotations for sermon writing.

THE ARMS TRADE

1. David Evans, "We Arm the World," *In These Times* (November 15, 1993), p. 14.

2. Quoted in "The Economics of Peace," *The New Yorker* (February 19, 1993). No page number and no author cited.

3. The Federation of American Scientists, in its *F.A.S. Public Interest Report* 45:6 (November/December 1992) notes that the U.S. has now "produced record U.S. arms transfers." This document contains many of the details and statistical facts appearing subsequently in this chapter. Another important source for such data is *The Defense Monitor* 21:5 (1992), published by the Washington-based Center for Defense Information.

4. Quoted in Editorial, *In These Times* (December 28, 1992), p. 2.

5. Evans, "We Arm the World," p. 17.

6. Ibid., p. 14.

7. "The Economics of Peace."

8. Michael T. Klare, "License to Kill," *In These Times* (January 10, 1994), p. 14.

9. Ibid., p. 17. Much in this paragraph is taken from Klare's fine article, which is the best treatment I have seen of the problem. Especially useful is his chart of countries, weapons, and other details, culled mainly from the *SIPRI Yearbook* and *Jane's All the World's Aircraft*, given the U.S. government's determination to keep official records on this subject classified.

10. Ibid., p. 15.

11. The Standing Commission on Peace filed a report on economic conversion, with relevant recommendations, with the General Convention of the Episcopal Church in 1991. It appears in the "Blue Book" for that convention, and constitutes a general background for the present writing on the topic.

12. Quoted in the 1991 "Blue Book" report to the General Convention by the Episcopal Church's Standing Commission on Peace.

13. Cited in the 1991 General Convention report.

14. Seymour Melman and Lloyd Dumas, *The Nation* (April 16, 1990).

15. Quoted in Evans, "We Arm the World," p. 17.

16. Ibid., p. 18.

17. Klare, "License to Kill," p. 19.

18. Evans, "We Arm the World," p. 16.

19. World Council of Churches, "Arms Transfers and Proliferation—Guideline for the Churches" (Geneva: Switzerland, December 1993).

A LEGACY OF MANIFEST DESTINY

1. Quoted in James B. Goodno, *The Philippines: Land of Broken Promises* (London and New Jersey: Zed Books, 1991), p. 32.

2. Ibid., p. 33

3. Michael McClintock, *Instruments of Statecraft: U.S. Guerilla Warfare, Counter-insurgency, and Counter-terrorism: 1940–1990* (New York: 1992), p. 125.

4. News Release: "A Statement on the Unabated Kidnap for Ransom and Senseless Killings." Executive Council, meeting on March 23 (1993?) in Baguio City.

5. Document of the Executive Council, Philippine Episcopal Church (April 6, 1992).

6. Editorial: "What Human Rights Violations?" *The Central Luzon Tribune* (January 1993).

7. Amnesty International, *Human Rights and US Security Assistance* (December 1992), p. 42.